SO THE STORY GOES

Edited by

Heather Killingray

First published in Great Britain in 2001 by
POETRY NOW
Remus House,
Coltsfoot Drive,
Peterborough, PE2 9JX
Telephone (01733) 898101
Fax (01733) 313524

HB ISBN 0 75432 664 0
SB ISBN 0 75432 665 9

FOREWORD

Although we are a nation of poets we are accused of not reading poetry, or buying poetry books. After many years of listening to the incessant gripes of poetry publishers, I can only assume that the books they publish, in general, are books that most people do not want to read.

Poetry should not be obscure, introverted, and as cryptic as a crossword puzzle: it is the poet's duty to reach out and embrace the world.

The world owes the poet nothing and we should not be expected to dig and delve into a rambling discourse searching for some inner meaning.

The reason we write poetry (and almost all of us do) is because we want to communicate: an ideal; an idea; or a specific feeling.

Poetry is as essential in communication, as a letter; a radio; a telephone, and the main criterion for selecting the poems in this anthology is very simple: they communicate.

CONTENTS

NOBODY KNOWS

A new breath breathed into her arms,
The baby she'd borne an hour before.
A handsome child from love had come!
But John had gone and not returned.
He'd died on foreign soil, interned by foreign hands.
She'd felt the babe was an extension of her John.
She fed and clothed him as he grew and learned,
But unlike John he did not nurture ways
Of love, but ones of hate. He stole
From all his friends, his mother too.
His little face grew greedy through the years,
Her dreams of little Johnny dashed away.
Nothing left of John, but love and dreams,
And Johnny always went his wicked ways
Her tears fell often on the barren soil
He trod and gradually her life slipped away.
A gentle lady came into his life
And changed his hard and greedy, grabbing ways.
With her he spent a rich and loving life.
Too late for her who'd loved him all those days!
He realised the faults of ill-spent youth
And knew too late for her he'd learned the truth!
Another little Johnny came along
And Johnny has his thoughts of things to come.

J E Blissett

MY CHOSEN THOUGHTS

A face blessed by natural beauty - with fine grace true
Many years have passed - and still that beauty can be seen -
even the ups and downs of life haven't taken away that fine grace -
and one is drawn by the value that they hold.

R P Scannell

WHO'S MY FATHER?

'Who's my father,
What's his name?
Do I bring him
Guilt and shame?
Does he love me,
Does he care?
Does he realise
Life's not fair?
Is he happy,
Living free?
Does he even
Know of me?'
All these questions,
All those lies
And in my arms
The young girl cries.

A J Hunter

BUSY WITH A HORSE

To own a horse,
What a course,
Through a leaflet,
Of items to buy,
I could adopt,
A horse.

He was lovely
Eating the grass,
He had been sick,
But the church,
Took hold.

It was a happy,
Time, until it,
Ran out, but,
He is well
Looked after,
I won't get
Another.

B Brown

GOING BACK

She stands by the gate her head bowed,
the old lady; her carriage proud.
Neatly gloved hand rests on the bar.
I sensed her thoughts have travelled far
back in time, erasing today,
ignoring the signs of decay
in her old home of many years;
trying hard to hold back the tears.
I wonder if she hears and sees
the visions of her family?
For sixty years they all lived there.
And now it's hard for her to bear
the move to council flat so trim
with lift and bell and nurses prim.
I offer her a cup of tea.
She turns around and comes to me.
I know exactly what she'll say,
'They're all so kind in every way -
    but it's not home dear.'

Marjorie Haddon

A WALK IN THE WOODS

I went for a walk in the woods,
I gazed at the trees and birds,
They spoke back and told me of wondrous things.
I listened with an attentive ear
Knowing there was something to learn.
They spoke of the truth,
They had no use for lies and deception,
They are at one with nature's ways.
They told me, the maker of themselves
Is also the same maker of my own being
And if I would but understand this
And expand my realisation of life's creation,
I would one day free my soul from the body
And all the illusions of falseness.

Well I left the woods and walked back to my home
With new hope in my heart and a divine feeling
Of Eternity.

Nick Purchase

LONDON'S PLAYING FIELDS FIASCO

Noted athletes used to train down
At Priest Hill, in Ewell, Surrey.
Linford Christie graced that small town.
Thompson, and John Barnes would hurry
To success, on eighty acres
Of sports ground, that's now in danger
From the building firms' plot-stakers.
Time's a negligent deranger

Of this game-selection park,
To which school teams came by bus.
What a sad end for this landmark.
Come on, sportsfolk, make a fuss!
New-Age travellers are a menace -
Squatting on your running tracks,
And the courts where you'd play tennis -
Without paying Council Tax.

Gillian Fisher

A SCHOOLBOY'S DREAM

Back of the classroom
In a world of his own
Close to the window, alone
Bustling white clouds are the ocean
Wild, frothing with white foam
Seagulls calling 'Come on!'
Surge of feeling takes him
Conjuring up a sailing ship
Wind whipping through his hair
Hoist the sails, breath salt air
Muscles straining, pull the ropes
Water spraying, drenching his skin
Hot sun bleaching his clothes
Bare feet running the boards
Captain orders 'Get below!'
Time for food, crowded galley
A banquet as much as he can eat
'Ahoy there,' waving at passing crews
Land ahead, desert island looms
Palm trees, brown-skinned girls
Paradise, dream brutality interrupted
'Where's your homework boy?'

Peggy Billett

FROM A DREAM TO A DREAM

I awake with his face
In the morning sun,
The shades in his features,
Bring about a smile,
Second to none,
The texture of his skin,
Entices me to reach out and touch,
His breathing shallows mine
As I want to Hush.
If I go to sleep and never awake,
I would call this
Destined fate.

Della Clark

WITNESS

Many stories link the ages
From the beginnings before time
In an unkind rhyme
In the many-coloured pages
Time we can no longer witness
The beauteous tree-clad earth
In latter days a dearth
The glorious flowers and animals to guess

Likewise the wavering foaming seas
Once leapt in life and sang
Their own song in the flow'ry tang
Now only pictures to please,
The air too with birds of flight
Or stranger animals we never knew
Passed unknown but with us grew
Their beleaguered cousins now near - past out of sight.

Past histories and sagas too oft' forgot
For the well-worn signs of times
In modern recorded pages mime
The savage human hand in our lot:
Each small animal that daily strives
To live as life but cannot flee
The terror of such a dynasty:
A kind hand to history, if past, to animals to add to
life and never deprives.

John Amsden

DREAMS

Ivory towers, confetti falls, dreams come true,
but not for me or for you!

Cracks appear, the mirror's shattered,
crumbling reality dawns.

A smack, a thud, the room vibrates
all over my body aches.

What did I do to deserve you?
I must be rotten through and through!

The punch bag's broke, I begin to choke
chained tight, but this can't be right!

Here I sit in my corner
Shivering, shaking, getting smaller.

Dark descends,
My lover's name never to defend.

Kyanne

HC TOWERS

Once I unearthed some old bottles and a pewter mug,
The mug had an inscription which read,
Presented to HC Davenport for service rendered,
To the RNLI and dated nineteen thirty-one,
Another inscription on the bottom read,
Good on you Charlie with the mark of the sun.

I cleaned up the mug and kept it for years,
Often wondering about HC and his exploits,
Then I met an old man of the sea in Poole,
He knew of Charlie when he was alive and well,
In fact across many an ocean they did sail.

Charlie, it appears, was a hero,
Rescuing countless people from the sea,
Never a thought for his own safety,
Always ready to take a chance, to save someone
                                    from a watery grave,
Even saved two young boys who were caught
                        by the rising tide in a rocky cave.

Charlie was colourful and flamboyant,
                            a real old character,
An old sea dog, the salt of the earth,
Everyone knew and had time for Charlie,
Apparently everywhere that Charlie went,
Laughter and joy were evident,

Then one day in the Second World War,
He was lost at sea, sunk by a U-boat's torpedo,
Left to rest in the sea he loved,
I tried to return the mug to Charlie's kith and kin,
But I couldn't trace anyone of his still living.

My treasure was unearthed from under an old shed,
On a disused allotment on which now stands,
A high-rise horror, stretching to the sky,
I nicknamed this high-rise block, HC Towers,
As a monument to Charlie, at which one a year I lay flowers.

P J Littlefield

LOVE'S LABOUR LOST

Recently,
Things seem to have changed,
Feelings no longer the same
As they once were.

Today,
In the morning
I thought let me make
An effort, a simple attempt,
To regain his attention and affection
A sacrifice, a beautification
Of what is clearly obvious,
To everyone but him.

Tonight,
I sit here,
Make-up smeared, tears streaming
Hair flying wildly in the wind,
Just like the tongues and fists
That were raised just moments ago,
Pen to paper
One last try,
To make clear what is apparent
. . . to bring him back home.

Farrah Mahmood

UP AND AWAY

Open wide the garage door, bring out the aero car
Put in some fuel pellets, for we're going very far
All tickets sold for Mars today, please don't look so sad
We'll go to Mars another day, today just to the moon
Pull the wheels up, secure them tight, we'll be there very soon
Put on the strap, pull it tight, for weightless we shall be
Press the start, set the course, for the Sea of Tranquillity
Safely landed, transfer quick, to a moonscape car
Bleak and rugged is the scene, viewed from near and far
Hurry to the city dome, where you can breathe with ease
Good atmosphere, sunny clime, complete with flowers and trees
Have a really smashing time, then go home for tea
Holiday on Mars this year? We shall have to see
Maybe we could take a cruise around the Milky Way
Then home in on Saturn to make a little stay
Maybe we could set the trend and stay on Earth this year
Something really old time, just sun, sea, sand and beer.

Dora Watkins

A SIMPLE TASK

Easy, simple task or so you would think,
As further down in my armchair I sink.
At eighty, standing up becomes a chore,
It often ends with me falling on the floor.

But, friends, I again go into the breach,
Withered joints stretched, chair arms I reach.
Now a downward push with force required,
While much stronger legs are what are desired.

One last effort and I am standing tall,
Ready to fetch post from box in hall.
Returning to safety of my soft seat,
Task accomplished, my story is complete.

S Mullinger

NO ESCAPE!

Sweat and tears were his armour-plate
over land baked dry with arid sun -
From Los Angeles to Mexico - ridge
with blistered feet he journeyed on.

Young dreams led him to the edge
where fanciful hopes of freedom lay -
So deeply baked in God's handiwork
his colour black was the cross he bore.

What cruel tricks the Hand of Fate
impede the Peace and Freedom sought -
The golden fleece beyond yonder sky
shattered by foreign lingo - *stop!*

Gutted with weariness and pain
near nigh dead yet his captives rage -
Their lingo not to his command -
Weary in body he's still the slave.

Handed back from whence he came
each day he fights for liberty -
A young life rots in St Quentin Jail -
His crime - mistaken identity!

Mary Skelton

FIELD OF OAK TREES

At the base of his tree, Gorf's in hibernation
He sleeps out the winter, snug in his den
Safe in the oak till spring comes around
Far away from the frost and winter blizzards that blow

A handsome young squirrel is out and about
Exploring his home from morning till night
At the edge of the forest a building he spied
A hut made of wood, with a chimney that smoked

On a notice he reads 'Private land' owned by the Sovereign
Field of Oaks, No Trespassing, what could it mean?
He must go and ask Boyce, the one who lives in Old Oak
This snowy owl of note that's big as an eagle.

Boyce looked at his friend, and ruffled his feathers
Did you not know, our forest is owned by the Queen?
She lives in the castle, close by the loch
A long way from here, in a place called Scotland

To hunt for some food, Oakley set out again
Thanking his friend, he waved him goodbye
He found berries galore, a beech tree with nuts
A pine tree with cones as big as his arm

Deep in the forest Oakley sat in his tree
Watching the deer and rabbits go by
How happy he was, to live in this forest
Protected by 'No Trespassing Please'.

Boyce called to his friend, as he flew past his tree
See you soon Oakley, I must catch fish for my tea
I am off to the lake to see what I can find
A beautiful bird, as white as the snow.

Oakley is tired, it's time for his bed
The sunset glows red, night clouds rolling in
He's had a long day, so much he has learned
He smiles to himself, tomorrow will be, a beautiful day
Goodnight everyone, goodnight.

Carole A Cleverdon

ROAD SERVICE

Blood-red, burnt and blackened,
Oozing liquid from the four shells within,
Incarcerated screams can be heard
Disturbingly agonized and fearful,

The images of the collision
Spinning through the air
Sparks crimson-red,
Adrenalin rushes the bodies now broken,
Lying on its roof, wheels whirring the
engine runs,

Sirens wail in the distance,
Help for these unfortunate few
The suffering cries for help die away,
Drowned out by the emergency services,

Cutting through blood-smeared metal aghast,
Three people pulled free and safe,
The car explodes into an inferno of flame,
Shattering flesh bloody and torn
Searing and burning wafting upon the
breeze,
The driver's fears gone in a flood of tears,

His life is lost
A shameful cost.

K M Clemo

ME NANA'S RAG RUG OF LIFE

The heavy oak rug frame me Granda made in the backyard
The hessian cloth were feed bags, begged from a local farmer
Me Nana would wash the hessian in the poss tub in the outhouse and
mangle it then hang it out to dry
I remember going to me Nana and Granda's house as a child,
sitting in front of an open fire with the small oven attached to the
side on one of me Nana's hooky mats
Playing with the large balls of fabric of half-inch cut cloth whilst me
Nana would cut up history
Me Granda would stitch the hessian onto the frames and then mark
the patterns onto the fabric
Coming from the Durham pit background the tradition of the rag rugs
were and are now legendary
Me Granda would mark the pattern using charcoal, then using
household implements, pots, pans, basins, he would mark intricate
patterns but it would always have to have a black border -
that was traditional
Then me Nana would hook her magic
She could tell the history of each piece of cloth
Some pieces she would caress as if looking back and remembering
I remember especially the dark colours, these were from me Granda's
work trousers
Every scrap of material was used, worked deftly into the rag rug
Even though me Granda's pit trousers were well-worn they would make
the traditional border so as to live again for tens of more years, even
after the pits closed and the communities died
After Granda retired and was moved to a cottage with a garden, he
would show his flowers and garden produce and win prizes
at local shows
His beloved dahlias - these were his passion
Me Nana would incorporate his flowers into the designs of the rugs
She loved bright pink
I never knew where she got the pink material from in those days

Granda would sometimes sit at one end of the frame,
me Nana at the other
Peace and harmony and love going into each stitch
I expect me Granda whilst holding the hooky in large,
callused, pit dust
ingrained hands would remember his days down in the bowels
of the earth
Whilst me Nana with frail, work-worn hands would remember the hours
of worry each day as she would wait until she heard me Granda coming
in at the back door, safe again for another day.
I now have the frame and the tools of me Nana and Granda
Although new to the tradition of rag rug making, I am proud to have
this heritage
These well-worn tools which have been handled through tears and love,
have made history and will live on.

Hilary Jean Clark

As White As Snow

I sat with Uncle Willett in the dappled light
beneath the orchard trees and listened to the tale he told.
On this hot still day he mopped his brow,
drank cold tea from a bottle, and related to me the
days of his youth.
He and his family had survived one of the hardest of winters
by eating snow, nothing but snow for weeks on end.
They grew up as thin as razor blades.
He was of the opinion that the world was growing soft
and doubted that we could survive the way they had.
He removed his brown felt hat and tugged at his white hair.
It had, he said, turned white from the snow that
he had eaten all those years earlier.
I knew my Uncle Willett to be the wisest man on Earth
And therefore believed every word that he told me!

Clive Cornwall

WATERMILL

Watermill, your wheel keeps turning,
Making the sparkling waters cascade,
In my dreams now all is gone, that mattered,
Memories - flow only of yesterday.

And like your wheel,
My mind's turning in never-ending circles,
    - forever in a spin,
And only with the wish of tomorrow,
Will hope, in my life again, be given
      the chance to win.

I placed my trust in good fortune,
That of which, I thought, I knew the best,
But fate again threw the dice,
And chance decided, that I had lost.

Now heartbreak, is my only companion,
That I once owned, is now, forever gone,
And watermill, like the waters, that share
With your paddles, only a short friendship,
The time, has come now too, for me to
      be moving on.

Bakewell Burt

WHY!

I sit and stare at the sky
thinking to myself, why, oh why
why these children wanted to see
that they were really hurting me

Four years of hell
and not a word
I kept myself quiet
that's what I preferred

I now live in Laxey,
with friends I'd like to keep
but my bullies still haunt me
in my sleep!

Siobhan Charnick

THE LAST STEAM TRAIN

Chasing across the countryside,
I saw the old train go,
Where its destination was,
I'm sure I do not know.

Smoke was pouring from its funnel,
The whistle sounded loud,
And all along the stations,
There was a mighty crowd.

The colours on that polished train,
Looked brilliant in the sun,
I bet it would look dusty
Before the day was done.

Faces peered out of the windows,
Hands waved as they all sped by,
Cars and bikes could not keep up,
However hard they'd try.

It was a really tragic day
When that steam train pulled its last,
We cheered, but cried for old times,
It whistled, then was past.

The diesel trains are nothing like
Those wonderful kings of steam,
Oh! How I used to envy,
The men who made their team.

Isobel Crumley

A TALE OF LIFE

You could gather all your thoughts
Into one long tale
A lovely day with babies small
Where happiness prevails
A special birthday
When the family all come round to tea
With presents wrapped
And coloured ribbons such a delight to see
Proud moments when your son and daughter
Suddenly are five
Going to school the joys encountered
Seems you'll reach the sky
In-between perhaps
You'll shed a tear for loved ones lost
The laughter comes into your life
Simply there because
A love surrounds your every day
To share in all you do
This lifetime is a wondrous tale
Of happenings for you.

Jeanette Gaffney

THINKING OF SLIMMING

I thought of going on a diet
To try and make myself thinner
I thought about having no breakfast
And not eating too much for dinner

But

When tea time came round I was starving
Although I am not one to boast
I ate two chicken legs, two scrambled eggs
And three or four slices of toast

Now, I don't think I'll go on a diet
Believe me it's not very funny
It's not very good, to go without food
And suffer hunger pains in your tummy.

Charles Staff

OUR JOURNEY A SUCCESS

I shall keep a diary
Of everything that happened on holiday
With my parents
On a boat
Cruising through
English countryside
No distractions
Just myself and them
Perhaps I should get away
To my cabin
To write my memoir
Although sometimes I see my parents
We adventurous three
Almost together
To aid my efforts
Of the pen
To write about our time
As some cathartic experience
My story of how we get along
Until we moor for the last time
The ending occurs to me
Fantastic, a work of art, I say
Do you want to read mum, I ask
'No' she says, 'Not really dear'
As we unpack the boat to return home
My story safe
Our journey a success.

C J Bayless

MATCH

Sitting in the shimmering heat,
Men in white clothes,
Tea in the pavilion,
Small sandwiches,
Scones, sunhats, packets of crisps.

Then applause, shouts from the field,
Scores going well,
Strong arm bowlers make ready,
Sweat shows through shirts,
The ball smacks against the bat.

Dresses and pretty suntops,
Summer sandals,
Canopies shading the prams,
Then photographs,
Cameras at the ready.

Community involvement,
Team spirit too,
Exercise, fresh air enjoyed,
Staunch supporters,
One afternoon in summer.

Kathleen Mary Scatchard

DEAR DIARY

As I grow up, year by year
My diary seems to grow with me
Never is an empty page spared
My writing is all that you see

Although my entries are few and far between
The emotions inside are not light
It offers me comfort in times of need
And I think about things when I write

Locked between the pages
Are my excitement and my fears
Though the ink may smudge or age
My memories will now stay for years.

Jenni Powner

AFTERNOON MEANDER

Come, take a stroll
In woodlands and meadows
Flowers are in bloom.
Trees 'dressed' in green.
Bird song, enchanting
We can stroll by the stream.
Perfect scene
A picnic spot
A 'place' for tots,
If no one is looking.
'Our age forgot'
A swing, can we remember
All the fun.
Then into the village
And bedecked, village green
Near the duck pond
And quaint, old church.
Tea rooms, still there
With windows tiny
Everywhere, bright and 'shiny'
Shall we call in,
For a nice pot of tea
I will have scones,
And your choice, my friend.
A wonderful day, nearing the end.
We must meet again soon
Before summer ends.

Margaret Parnell

A Bird On Wing

Come out, see it up there
As it flies through the air.
All silver in colour
It leaves a trail in the sky
As it flies by.
It glides down to the ground,
And slows right down to a standstill
No sound.
It's a beauty, I call it 'Babe'
Its beak is long and straight
When people know it's time for
                    it to be about
Many of them get their binoculars out
My 'Babe' looks so beautiful
Way up high,
Just see how it soars,
Downward from the sky.
Then watch it land,
It looks so grand,
My silver-coloured 'Babe'
                    Concorde!

Marion Staddon

Tribute To A Friend

Here lies a true and loyal friend
His days as my helper have come to an end
He worked for me in upland and bog
And was really special yet only a dog.

When I'd go to the town for me he would wait
Lying there patiently at our front gate.
And when I'd return I'd know without fail
He'd be there to greet me with a wag of his tail.

Wherever I went he was by my side
My feelings for him were of friendship and pride
When he got ill I felt very low
For deep down I knew it was his time to go.

When I found him dead at our front door
I knew my friend would be with me no more
I feel very sad for my dog has now gone
But one thing I know his memory lives on.

Dickie Anderson

THE COLLIE

As the swallows took to the air over the cricket pitch -
You followed, foolishly hoping, no doubt, to catch them,
Or, at the very least, to round them up, and marshall them
Into the imaginary fold of sheep that is your reason for being.
You chased the birds, and scattered them,
Until your owner whistled, and you returned,
Ever obedient and willing to please.
But, part-puppy that you are -
Some half-remembered, long-ago-given command got the better of you
And you returned to wildly chase the uncatchable swallows,
As they darted over the fields.
We watched you as you tried to encircle them,
Order them and coax them into the sheep-pen
That surely exists for ever in the collective unconscious of sheep-dogs -
Then, as we laughed, and your owner whistled once more,
The swallows returned to their nests -
And you to your owner's feet, and your life's dreams . . .

Jenny Proom

THE BEAUTIFUL FLAMINGOS

A venture of magnificence lay before me
The view from my plane window showed promise
I could hardly bear the wait
My plane landed safely at the airport

Fellow travellers chatted together about the venture
Its success depended on the sharp eyes of the beholder
Flamingos Island was just a boat ride away
The sight of coral pink creatures filled us with
      great pleasure

We landed on the leeward side of the island
And hiked to a positive position
Where we could view and not be seen
Complete silence filled us with awe at the beauty
      before us

Flamingo couples were courting and behaving serenely
Whist the younger ones amused themselves
Strutting around like lords of the sea
The dance they were performing completely
      dazzled us

Some flamingos took to the air
Their wing span gave them
The look of stately pink ships
Gliding aimlessly, over the starry sunlit sea

Suddenly, the sky was full of a gliding pink cloud
Eggerton had broken the silence
He sneezed out loud, to cause this dilemma
The sadden struck man apologised profuscly

The pink cloud of flamingos
Hovered backwards and forwards over the island
It was no use watching anymore
So back to our boat, the oarsman rowing, we fled
    into the starlit night

Alma Montgomery Frank

THE GIRL AT WORK

Four years ago I left my wife
I wanted to live a better life
You see I'd fallen in love with the girl at work.

I told lies to the wife and made her cry
She was so unhappy she wanted to die
Because I'd fallen in love with the girl at work.

I rented her a house fit for a queen
She didn't want me I felt so green
I thought she loved me the girl at work.

I lived in that house all on my own
The happiest time I'd ever known
Because in my dreams I loved the girl at work.

My wife wanted me back to try again
But she couldn't forget the grief and pain
Because I still love the girl at work.

The fighting became worse
My wife does shout and curse
All because I love the girl at work.

I don't love the wife the time has gone
It's time to say goodbye - so long
All because I do know I love the girl at work.

Muriel Turner

A WARTIME EVENT

Somehow we surmounted restrictions and difficulties of
                              wartime movements
An unexpected opportunity to leave behind the wartime
                              horrors and torments

Early autumn, six days holiday in far off Cornwall's beautiful Newquay
How we longed to breathe the clear air and perhaps bathe
                              in the blue sea

Found suitable and affordable pleasant room in quiet seaside hotel
Guaranteed a few good night's sleep in comfort for a spell

On the first evening we strolled along the seashore
Deserted we thought at first but oh dear no more

Surprised, a little flattered by the friendly if cheeky greeting
From a couple of lads in Airforce blue very keen on a meeting

Stuart and Bobby, Air Cadets on an evening pass that day
Freed from flying training at a station not too far away

Seemed they were flying the Tiger Moths and such like training planes
Later they would both be sent overseas to learn to fly Spitfires
                              and Hurricanes

We four met on several occasions enjoying each other's company
Walking, talking, laughing and the usual tom foolery

Such pleasantries and happy memories are still with me today
For many long years I was in friendly contact with Bobby Gray
Long letters, aerograms, postcards and such from the USA

Too late to fly fighters in the Battle of Britain
Plenty of action from D Day landings in Europe that was certain

Demobbed Bobby returned to Edinburgh University
Graduating with an Honours Masters Degree

A Professor in Medicine Hat, Canada and later in the USA
Seemed settled, happy and successful in every way

Letters arrived less frequently, then no more for a year I would say
Eventually news arrived from his mother in Edinburgh to say

My son Bobby is now a Buddhist Monk in a Californian Monastery
His parents and I knowing Bobby so well found this action
                                                a complete mystery

K G Johnson

THE STRANGER

As night approaches
I see a man waiting
at the bottom of our garden

It grows dark
and still he waits

'Why don't you go out
and speak to him?' my wife says

I am afraid to admit to her my fear
I open the door
and take a couple of steps outside

The man turns toward me in silence
His eyes shine like wet leaves
His face is stained by the stars
I cannot speak

From the house
I hear footsteps and my wife's whisper
'It's late - please . . .'
And I leave him there
and lock the door behind me . . .

In the first light of morning
I see where the grass is
strangely flat and bare

Ian Seed

THOSE WERE THE DAYS

Something that you hear
It is a common phrase
Take a look back in time
Because 'Those were the days'
When tin baths were used
One washed, who was next?
Hand-me-down clothes
No talk about sex
'Run for the shelter!'
The siren is crying
Hiding in the darkness
Whilst the soldiers are dying
No video players
Hardly ever saw a car
No expensive posh pets
Just a tadpole in a jar
There were marbles and jacks
Porcelain dolls, hopscotch too
A seat in the flea pit
Cost a shilling or two
Mrs Dales Diary on the wireless
Bag of coal for the fire
Squeeze the washing through a mangle
To the laundrette for a washer and dryer
Chicken once a year at Christmas
Plain crisps with a bag of salt
There were steam trains and trams
Kodak box cameras - front doors without bolts
Black polish on hobnailed boots
No GCSEs, for us - eleven plus
Pack of ten woodbines
A conductor on the bus
A guinea or a threpence

Quill pens you dipped in ink
Best clothes on a Whitsun
Pigtails with ribbons of pink
An annual trip to somewhere
It was all we could afford
Bags of chips and some scrumpy
We were happy, never bored
No talk of the ozone layer
We had lots of the sun's rays
Families were big and we were poor
We didn't care because those were the days!

Joanne Hale

ONE VIOLET

Pictures are painted
Epics voiced
Vast musical scores are measured
We view, we listen
And mostly, like Morris dancers
We stomp through the experience
Or, holding tightly to our ribbon
We join the rest
Circumnavigating the Maypole.
Let go the ribbon
Slip off the shoes and pause
For all the great
Is mirrored in the small -
The panoramic view
In what the fingers touch
And one bird's song
One bloom's perfume
Is grace enough.

Norah Mitchell

GHAZAL: BEGINNINGS

I stand on the rim of the sea looking out
At the incoming waves like a *tabula rasa.*

After the siren, among a flood of overalls,
How to distinguish particular from general blue?

Why did the man enquire if I could read?
Were they illiterate, those children of the sea?

Euclid and Pythagoras got their comeuppance
From the sinuosities of *The Song of Solomon.*

Marching to worship and a psalmody of tears,
In that inglorious tradition an alien interloper.

Chaucer was there at the beginning, together with
The Wanderer and *The Vision of the Cross.*

Bright as a sparrow on the retreating platform,
Her wave a compound of encouragement and grief.

No confidence that I could harness beauty,
Until I recognised equal and matching goodness.

Our marriage archway boasted: 1496 -
The year Columbus left Hispaniola and returned to Spain.

Bless Pumpernickel's rendering of Scott
(Knowledge of German, French and Latin being prerequisites).

Fate found me in Jerusalem, minus my better self,
The day they christened me: *Abu Dawud.*

Outside a clinic door in Ankara, I heard
The birth cry of a vagabond romantic gourmet lawyer.

And slipping from Plaça Nova into La Seu
I prayed: Madonna and the precious Trinity.

The toad hopped off into the undergrowth.
Then, hand-in-hand, we took the path for Xanadu.

So many old beginnings, new beginnings
The withdrawing waves wipe gently from the shore.

Norman Bissett

MORNING TIME

Morning Time!
A small sure voice pre-empts the dawning light
Morning time, it's morning time
I've slept all through the night
I've put my Womble slippers on
Mr dressing gown as well
I've ready my Andy Pandy books
And I've rung my garage bell
I turned my wireless fully on
And other noisy tricks
Like banging shut my wardrobe doors
Just to hear the clicks
I've played with Daddy's pennies
In the little glass ashtray
And I've pulled on Mummy's ticking clock
Till the handle came away
I've emptied all the cuff links
That were in my daddy's drawer
I've torn up all the tissues
And had a look for more
I want some juice and biscuits
To fill my hungry tummy
But hush! - my daddy's fast asleep
So I think I'll wake up Mummy

Ray Ryan

I AM THE PRINCESS LIVING IN LONDON

She shook me awake, she couldn't
let me sleep.

The husband hoovering and whistling
long thin arms folded across his chest.

I vanish and I return.
White hot.

It feels like
Maralinga.

I wrote it as she told me to
the best of my ability although

- *What is this ju-ju?*
No one knows.

The husband and son booked in for London.
The husband too - what's the word?

Traditional - to take a hotel room until
2pm check in on the day of arrival.

- *We'll snooze in Westminster Abbey*
like I always do.

We turn on the TV.
I can't remember why.

The photo with two dates
that you get when you die.

Arc you still with mc?
Do you know what comes next?

The husband and son landed in London
the day of the funeral and of course

they couldn't get near
Westminster Abbey.

From what they said later
I knew where they were.

The moment you weren't sure
which way the crowd would go.

And they went under the Channel
to Paris and sighted the tunnel.

Where it was cold, no doubt, cold.
Cold in the tunnel.

Jennifer Compton

MY DOG

You burst into our lives
It seems like yesterday.
Bedraggled and determined
Your eyes begged 'Let me stay.'
Many years have passed since then.
You helped us along the way.
You loved and laughed, brought comfort too
And how you loved to play
The brightness of those loving eyes
The smile that seemed to say,
'I'm glad it's you I chanced upon,
That sad and desperate day.'
I see your smiling face
It's saying 'Don't despair'
The love we had between us still
               lingers in the air.
Just close your eyes, I'm with you still
I loved you then, and,
               timeless, always will.

Gladys Mary Gayler

THE TASTER

The wine glass pivoted centre stage
large and tulip - shaped
it's fine, clear glass balanced on a
slender stem, like a ballerina on pointe,
waiting for fulfilment.

Then a gentle creak and a pop
of a cork being pulled
was heard in the wings
It was the moment when the audience
became silent and the evening began.

This was an overture to a celebration.

The wine glass tilted against the white
back-drop allowing its audience
to enjoy the freedom of colours
within the wine.

A wine whose silkiness of texture
no other could emulate
Soft, red and juicy
whose aroma filled the stage
and fired imaginations of winter evenings.

Heart-warming, gloriously rich flavours
of fruit berries, black pepper and
dense, rich chocolate
perhaps even a whiff of smoke
A wine warm enough to be
flavoursome yet cool enough to be
refreshing.

Too soon it was time to drink
The finale began with sweetness
and ended with bitterness
Enjoying the personality and flavour
that the fumes imparted,
the maestro 'chewed' the wine
- then swallowed, satisfied.

His performance was over.

Jennifer Polledri

MY MOTOR CAR

My motor car is my
Prison-house
I shall not want
It maketh me to break down
On tarmacadamed motorways
It leadeth me into
Interminable cul-de-sacs
It destroyeth my soul
Yea, though I drive
Through the Valley of the Shadow of Death
I shall run out of petrol
The walker and the jogger
Overtaketh me
Surely MOTs and services
Shall follow me all the days
Of my life
And I will dwell in the
Garage of the Lord
Forever.

J C Crowe

CITY NIGHTS

The siren blasts at your mind,
You're lost in the headlights,
The taste of his lips corrupt your mind,
How the street clings to your soul,
How the tambourine licks your precious heart,
Photos of the love to grow, overtake your heart,
Drowning in your sorrows, safe out at sea,
Lying by her side, a place you dream to be,
For his taxi lifestyle brakes in your direction,
Strong, stronger than before,
But you're floating on heavenly water now,
Feel the salt kiss your eyes better,
You feel cleansed,
But you're not really here,
The man on the doorstep, playing his only tune to your restless ears,
The thumping of workers suits at the end of the day
Crashing at the pavement,
How the world seems to be so quiet from inside the glass,
Your safety in the control of a man dying
To keep his family above water,
Your tip brings a smile to his face,
Another year on your notebook,
What traps lie for you to get hooked onto?
Her brown eyes commit suicide,
Her face cuts through your back like a knife,
For a little world opens a new chapter in your heart,
For you to find a true love, to stop drifting apart,
Clenching onto your bags of decay,
The bus is full yet again,
You take a walk into his carriage,
A place you thought you'd never find him,
The deep sighs of a busy day echo through the train subway,
Reflections of his face in your eyes,
Makes your heart bleed to death, not to your surprise,
You laid your bed, so lay in it,

You set the stone, the path guided for you,
The sirens cry out your name,
For your heart carried to A + E,
The taste of your crying coul, open to the eyes of you and me,
The crashing of doors,
The tears in your eyes,
The love you had, now sliding doors close,
Your veins tangled in the transport system you become disillusioned,
Parked on your sofa bed,
The night clock just above your head,
The red digits counting down till your next day of despair,
City days, city nights,
Your heart, you thought were cleansed,
But we all knew that was a lie.

Warren Smith

A TREE IN WINTER

One winter day I walked a muddy footpath
mired with well-trod leaves under a sodden sky.
The day was monochrome, grey on grey.
An old tree, bare and bony, loomed out of a lowering sky,
its paltry seed pods pending in the demi-light.
And in the west the sky unclosed. Only a crack in the time
and space, but in one moment all that streaming light poured in.
The tree was a Chinese painting; dazzling pendants,
gleaming gold, hung from elaborate dragon shapes
on a ground of lapis and kingfisher.

A glimpse, and it was gone.
Now I am one who has been struck by light,
and live my life in hope that light may strike
in the same place twice.

Pat Mitchell

JOURNEY TO JAMAICA

Making sure all bags are packed,
all rooms are clean before we leave,
jump into our space cruiser,
taking the last look at our area.

Off we go to the airport,
there we sat thinking good and bad thoughts,
what is it going to be like,
what parties take part at night.

Finally the plane arrives,
as we enter the plane,
it starts to pour with rain,
our hearts pounding wishing we never came.

As we took off,
our ears started to pop,
get comfortable in our seats,
start to stretch out our feet,
whilst we got offered food to eat,
tired and exhausted so we went to sleep,

On the inside looking out,
felt as if we were flying through the clouds,
an eight hour journey,
wishing and wishing we get here early.

Landing In Jamaica

As the plane was about to land,
all the passengers screamed and clapped their hands,
hollering 'We've reached, we've reached.'

As we come off the plane,
no more horrible rain,
the sun was beaming hot!
We had to strip down into our little tops.

We stood waiting in a long queue,
waiting for our luggage to come through,
the Jamaicans on the other side of the gate,
saw the English girls and couldn't wait.

We met the family,
and went to the family car,
as we were driving down the street,
we heard the loud reggae beats,
we could smell Jerk chicken,
so we had to stop, it was finger lickin'.

Jamaica, Jamaica,
how beautiful could it be,
sunshine every day, sailing along the sea,
plenty of fruits to eat, ripe from the tree,
oh isn't Jamaica a wonderful place to be,
jump on a plane today then you can see.

Shantel Faure (17)

BEREFT

One of them died.
   There is a sort of absence
   A cold space, waiting -
While the sere leaves rattle on the scrub oak tree.

One of them died.
   There is a ringing silence
   Emptiness everywhere -
A lone seagull screams, cleaving the sky.

It was then I cried -
   It was just like that -
      When one of us died.

G Poole

GETHSEMANE'S GLORIOUS BATTLE

Give to dark Gethsemane weeping
Grief to the dark olive trees lent,
The form of the human Jesus,
Battling forces destruction-bent.

Earth's drinking His agonised blood-drops
Reddening its soil at those who keep
With Him His last vigil,
Forgot their Master in sleep.

He's battling with forces of evil
No mortal has ever yet met
Would you not spare Him a moment
To wipe His brow, red bloodstained sweat?

He's fighting for you this great battle,
He's suffering for you hour by hour,
O! Sinner, He's writhing, struggling
To conquer sin's strangling power.

His battle was won through the travail
Will love see you at heaven's gate?
His heart pleads with yours, time lingers,
One day soon it will be too late!

Alice Blackburn

DEDICATION

Once, I shone in the vale where souls are made,
My poems flowed as easily as breath,
But the tyrant Time too soon consigned my gift
To slow, slow death.

Once, divine music echoed in my soul,
With ease light's lilting rhapsodies unfurled,
But when Time slay the gift, I entered in
A bleak, bleak world.

At length, I reached the nadir of despair.
But it was there like an angel of fire you came,
Kindling my spark that fast was turning grey
To bright, bright flame.

Essence of Eden, Song of Paradise,
To you I write my stanzas of delight
Who took me from the dark and empty void
To the far, far light.

Pamela Constantine

ADVICE

Why complain of a sheltered flat?
Make it homely and bright.
If there aren't enough cupboards
Give things away, that's right!
You can't take it with you.
We all know that's true.
If the flat's too warm, you can't turn it round
If you could, it might be too chilly.
You could sit in the lounge;
Perhaps have a chat.
Don't write for a transfer or anything silly.
There's a seat in the garden to rest,
On a hot day, that's best.
If you have to share a WC
Or a bathroom, don't get blue.
Try to be good neighbours
You're unlikely to find a queue.
If a better home you'd like to find
Wait for the council to make up their mind.

E M Apps

BEYOND THE SHORE

Barefoot on a sandy shore,
Salty grit slithering through my toes,
Unbalanced by quick sand holes,
Squeaking gulls landing in pools,
Dreaming and gazing towards the horizon,
Mindful of its strength to surprise one,
Moving shades of green and blue,
Frilly, frothy, white edging accrues,
Powerful action showing its means
Its never failing speediness reigns supreme.

Barefoot on a sandy shore,
Light fading fast, to conceal,
Visual art of all that is real,
Only sounds can be heard in the dark,
Of waves pounding on groans of bark.
And shifting sands shuddering on the shore,
Making one mindful of the power it stores.

Barbara R Lockwood

TALES OF BEATRIX POTTER

Sketches of animals were portrayed in her drawings
Inspirational moments that captured the greenery
Where Lakeland hills interweaved with the flora
Against a background of beautiful scenery

The familiar characters she had come to know
In daily pursuit of ideas became habit
This young woman found, her friends closer to home
Furry animals included a character named Peter Rabbit

Where toadstools and trees and fictional ducks
Were brought to life, by a story on a page
Cherished friends as pets, never to be plucked
Those fairy-tale illustrations that signified a past age.

Rebecca E Humphrey

SCARLET RIBBONS

There's a bonny moorhen on the shore by the sea
Where willows weep and time leaves me
To do the things that life has left
To climb up the rocks in the nooks and clefts.

And you pick up a scarlet ribbon
The like of which you've never seen,
And you wonder if you're still awake
Or if this is all a dream.

There's a golden goosie nesting in the meadow
Where the grass is green and the air is heavy with dew,
And life has left me here
With not a single thing left to do.

And you see a silver sunrise
That is appearing in the east,
And now the goosie's flown away,
But the wood nymph's still here at least.

So you lay down in the tall grass
Where grasshoppers click and honey bees hum,
And all your dreams are of scarlet ribbons
Though you've never seen the like of one,

And when day is done and a new moon is full
But later, much later when even night is past
In the depths of your mind, in the hours no one sees
You'll awake to find your scarlet ribbons at last.

E Marshall

STEPHANIE'S CHILD

'I The Lord created you
I named you to be mine;
You are dear and precious,
Loved with my love divine.

A tiny pulse, a thread of life,
barely perceptible on the scan,
yet as we watched in awed delight
we beheld the forming of a man.

Too tiny for the naked eye to see,
so fragile in its form;
just settled in a womb of love,
waiting to be born.

There we beheld the miracle,
the miracle of life;
a new creation formed by God
for a daughter and a wife.

Thank You Lord for this precious gift,
for new birth once again;
and thank You that we are dear to You,
and called by Your own name.

Catherine Riley

H IS COMPLAINING!

Basking in sunshine; like a relaxed cat
Across carpet from the French Window mat -
Alert to the garden birds he barks at!
Stirs to chase field mice who came to squat.

Then food-wise he likes turkey and chicken
But sits up to beg for favourite salmon!
Sits on lap, zealously licks hand: 'Come on
Silly, stroke my fur, you lazy human!'

As small as a feline with yapping bark
This canine is his master's pet. Then dark
Of thunderstorm's cloud claps - it's raining:
Cloudburst of cats and dogs yet H is complaining!

Suzanne Stratful

THE DECADE OF YEARS

Listening to another world,
Hunger and destruction
Earthquakes, floods, starvation, HIV
Leaves little hope, for regeneration

Little child clings to a mother breast
Nothing there, to satisfy
Keeping warm, not realising
Not very long for it to die

Worrying times, please find a reason
For people so poor, a way of life
Eating rice, a staple diet
Very little food, to survive

Why is the world, so divided
In the millennium, we talk of hope
Charities seem to help a little
Excited faces, on the little folk

We can only hope and pray
Little else that we can do
Hoping God can make the changes
Listening to our prayers, from me, and you

Decades have passed, with little change
Poverty, it is, still there
You'd think, in this new millennium
We all would get, an equal share

Florrie MacGruer

WAR

There are men all around carrying guns
A woman I know lost both her sons
My daddy is dead and my mummy is sad
So my brothers and I aren't being bad
I'm so frightened and so are the others
The children around me stay close to their mothers

We are on the move now so I hope we will soon be safe
I know now I will have to be brave
Mummy said I was a big boy now
I've got to look after my brothers
But I don't know how

She was there yesterday but today she's not
All I have left is a teddy I brought
My brother won't stop crying
He said he saw mummy dying
Running down his cheeks are lots of tears
And behind those eyes are all the fears

A kind man took us along with him
He said 'Don't be scared my name is Tim'
We flew to a place far away
Which is now our home and we love to stay

My mum and dad are stars in the sky
Every night they pass us by.

Zoë Thompson

CHRISTMAS 1944

No jingle-bells, but the sound of sirens,
No sweet song of Silent Night,
But the droning roar of bombers fast approaching.

Run children, run - run for shelter -
She clutched the baby, stumbled, fell.
The skies ablaze with flares the bombers dropped,
Before they hit their target - the innocent.

Anne Marie Frazer

HORSES

See those beautiful horses grazing in the field,
On the lush green grass that the good earth doth yield,
Some of them are brown, some dapple grey and some white,
And some of them fawn, such a wonderful sight.

Those horses are so peaceful and without a care,
So much of their time spent out in the fresh air,
As they are meandering around in company,
With each other, and in complete harmony.

All of them are so graceful, lithe and handsome too,
Grazing the green grass is the most that they do,
But sometimes they stand still or they canter about,
Always seem so contented, there is no doubt.

And when they feel tired they lie down on the green grass,
With sweet dreams and careless of how time does pass.
Then quite soon they will rise up from where they have lain,
Start grazing the green grass all over again.

Their lovely long tails are swishing from side to side,
And people on their backs will aspire to ride,
We must look on them all with great admiration,
As part of our God's wonderful creation.

See those beautiful horses grazing in the field,
On the lush green grass that the good earth doth yield,
But when the cold, storm and snow comes, then they will all,
Be tucked up warm and comfy in a clean stall.

Ruth Dewhirst

MY BIRTHDAY 2001

This year my birthday was special
and here's the reason why.
My first granddaughter entered this world,
Oh the joyous tears I did cry.

You see she was ten weeks early,
and weighing just over two pounds,
but her look of determination
and the strength to live she found.

Although she is very tiny,
she is perfect in every way.
She looks at you with open eyes,
saying 'Yes I'm here to stay'

Oh the love and joy I feel,
when I cradle her in my arms,
if only her grandad was here today,
he too would fall for her charms.

Already her own personality is present
as each day goes by.
Yes, my birthday this year was special,
because Lara Louise you're the reason why.

Yvonne Lewis

MY BABY- FOR DARRAN (BORN 22.01.69)

I have a little baby, who sucks his toes and hands,
When I give him my fingers, he straightens, then he stands,
He bites and chews on anything, that's left within his reach,
From baby sounds to little words, I now begin to teach.

He's just six months, and growing fast, and always on the go,
Himself, and all his family, he really seems to know,
He looks into the mirror, and smiles a knowing smile,
He rolls onto his tummy, and likes to lie awhile.

He really is so beautiful, he is my pride and joy,
I am so very happy, I had a baby boy,
My family is now complete, I have a 'pigeon pair',
When happiness was given out, I really had my share.

Sheila Bates

LULLABIES

Will they sing
Sad songs
(Do they sing
Them now?)
In broguish tones
With strident strum
Of simple souls
Lost to a cause
Against power's
Unilateral right
To injury, injustice
And the like?

Will the lilting
Balladeers -
Oblivious or no -
Evoke a dreamy
Afterglow
In mind's eye,
Which commends
(Even as their
Rhymes condemn)
The cruel course
From then
To here?

Stephen H Hogg

DREAM POWER

Charlie had always wanted to ride a rollercoaster,
he had listened many times to other kids boast.
The thrill, the buzz, the screams and excitement,
he could only imagine, what their delight meant.

Consider thrills, the feeling of fun and fear,
as the highest point, slowly draws near.
Anticipate the pace, as the drop began,
feel the sweat, in the palm of his hand.

Experience his own body, being thrown about,
share sensations, as kids scream and shout.
Greet gravity, with a twisted smiling face,
retain good memories, of an exciting place.

Be out and about in the early summer sun,
spending a whole day, having nothing but fun.

But he'd never been, because his parents finances
were constantly in the red, but even so . . .
such was the power of his dreams,
he would frequently, fall out of his bed.

Mandy Ann Cole

THE BEGINNING OF THE END

As she holds me near
I know she's my sweetheart
I'm losing her I fear
We are growing apart

I know I love her, but
We have nothing in common
This is my first cut
But my heart is very solemn

I shall soon move away
And leave her behind
But we shall meet again
Hopefully better timed

I miss her so much
When she's not around
Her kind and gentle touch
And her soft warbling sound.

Danny Hopwood

COME HOLD MY HAND!

'Come, hold my hand!' the angel said, 'I'll lead you to a land
The Chosen Few alone must tread the day they understand
That God is love and so much more than human souls could sense
The day they open up the door. Forgiven. Now His friends.'
And so the angel led me there and proved my gallant guide
As I intently spoke a prayer, yet stared, eyes open wide!
'Behold the Tree of Life God made so many years ago!
Behold the ancient leaves that fade and yet by faith they grow!
Behold God's rainbow-like raptures 'twixt Heaven and the Earth!
How beautiful their light captures His holiness and worth!
Behold God's mountain borne of gold - its glory shames the sun!
Yet it's as nothing to Christ's fold - God's Shepherd loves each one!
Behold God's angels soaring high in perfect unison,
Their energy is God's supply - His gift to every one!'
'These sights,' I said, 'are not enough! It's Jesus I would see!
For Jesus is the Lord I love! The King of Calvary!
I've felt each blow, His cross of woe, six hours 'neath the sky!
I only know, I love Him so, who for my soul would die!'
The angel said, 'Your heart speaks true! I'll lead you to His Throne!
The day of death I'll fly you to the final vision shown.'

Denis Martindale

HORSES

When I find time I love to go a'rambling for pleasure,
Many horses do I meet usually taking their leisure.
From little pit ponies - who are often grey,
But can no longer work as they have had their day,
To the kingly shires - who are usually black,
One look at them tells you that they nothing lack.
They are dressed up to kill each and every day,
Yes, even though they've had their hay day,
Then there are what I call the in-betweens,
Their owners are usually kings and queens.
They are very docile and these days are often brown,
Especially when they are fully grown.
They are all lovely fellows with very doleful eyes
But like you and me they do love a snack of a carrot as a surprise.
Ask the owner first - for they could say yea or nay,
There could be something wrong with their digestion at a later day.
Quiet demeanour with a gentle word,
And you'll have them eating out of your hand like the smallest bird.

Betty Green

CASTLES IN THE AIR

Where's that idea leading you,
Up the garden path?
Hope you're watching,
Eyes right down,
Place your feet - neat,
Not to wander over the edge
Into the undergrowth
Which trips you up
And shows your scheme
For what it's worth -
A dream.

Just visions floating, bobbing about
On air above your mind.
They walk before you,
Leading you on
But do beware there's not another
Dreamer as daft as you,
You may collide
With opposing schemes
Marching down the garden path.

Brenda Dove

BEST CHEAP AND BEST CHOICE
(From Margaret Paston's letter 1449)

Dame Margaret Paston wrote the words five centuries ago,
   From Norfolk to her husband John who would to London go.
'To make me a hood' - for feasts, no doubt she needed finer stuff
   Than home-spun, which she'd spin and weave, for week days,
                              good enough.

A yard of broadcloth, black, she asked, his good wife Margaret,
   From Hays' wife, or so she'd heard, best cheap and best choice
                                   he'd get.
'44 pence or four shillings a yard', a bargain price, no doubt
   From Hays' wife of London, not too hard to seek her out.

She asked her John crossbows to buy to guard against attack,
   If rival claimants took to force before her lord came back.
And other stuff for children's gowns, sugar and almonds too,
   A pound of each - though she'd bad news she made but small ado.

The folk who claimed John Paston's house in ale house had been heard
   Plotting attack - Dame Margaret knew - John's men told every word -
Undauntedly her watch she'd keep -
   But still she wanted broadcloth, cheap!

Kathleen M Hatton

SIR STANLEY SPENCER, 1891-1959

Nestling in a haven, in Cookham rural Berkshire,
Was born a visionary artist, whom the populous admire.

He was born on Cookham High Street, surviving child eight,
Revered as one of last century's most original is his fate.

Educated by his sisters in the Fernlea garden shed,
The son of a piano teacher, whom an eclectic life has led.

For his personal life was fraught, dual affections caused him strife,
Hilda beloved, constant, then his lascivious second wife.

Staunch patriotic feeling amidst the First World War,
In Bristol and Salonika served the Army Medical Corps.

A world-renowned artist, nurtured by the Slade,
Meticulousness in drawings has an English painter made.

Acute attention to detail, child-sized brushes he did use,
Enabled biblical scenes with Cookham countryside to fuse.

He depicted daily life and in Cookham based much matter,
Swan Upping, The Resurrection, Christ Preaching at the *Regatta.*

Ecumenical fervour, pot boiler landscapes divine,
War, nudes, shipbuilders, rounded figures his style define.

His large *shipbuilding series* in Port Glasgow on the Clyde,
Portrays the artisans' work, harsh reality does not hide.

A sanctuary to Art, the 'Church-House' was his vision,
But against the flow of time, never came into fruition.

Unlike Sandham Memorial, war scenes emblazoned head to toe,
Commissioned at Burghclere Chapel in the style of Giotto.

Map reading and bed making, here are subjects on display,
And the soldiers' resurrection with their crosses whence they lay.

He was a true eccentric, his pram chassis served him fine,
Transporting his materials and 'Do not disturb me' sign.

He summarised in three choice words *'A wonderful desecration'*,
Five decades of his work, which do still delight our nation.

Written as his life extinguished, *'Sorrow and sadness is not for me'*,
His tombstone stands for all to hail the Spencer legacy.

Jennifer Brookes

WINTER'S NIAGARA

Graceful, glacial curtains,
imprison,
Niagara's thunderous cascades.
Diamonds, sapphires, topaz,
multi-faceted slivers,
flicker dance, within ice,
in pirouetting profusion,
'neath winter's afternoon glow.

White, icy froth,
suspend,
frigid frozen poses.
Icicle latticework awaiting,
in patient surveillance,
spring's gentle thaw, creak and sigh,
as fabulous falls roar,
a resounding scream for release.

Sun's tender kiss,
liberates,
Niagara's torrential falls.
Shattered, water-ice ruptures,
mini icebergs, crash.
Freed, once again, frolicking,
flooding river, sings,
in joyous inspiration.

P Davies

CAN YOU
ADAM AND EVE IT?

I once read the bible
From one end to the other
A mystery within its leaves
Soon would I discover.

It starts when God made Adam
Earth's first and only man
From Adam's rib he then made Eve
And that's how life began.

Adam, he made love to Eve
From this there came two sons
The bible then made me believe
That they were the only ones.

Abel was their good son
A kind and loving boy
But Cain he was a bad son
Was the Devil he'd employ.

Poor Abel he was murdered
By his brother, evil Cain
Abel's soul cried out to God
'By my brother's hand I'm slain.'

With great anger our Lord God
Put a mark on evil Cain
He banished him to the Land of Nod
Saying 'Don't come back again.'

When Cain arrived in the Land of Nod
He fell in love and wed
This was where with the Book of God
I began to lose my head.

The Bible says that God has made
One man, one woman, that's two
Then together they made two sons
And one got wed - to who?

Marie Horridge

DOWN BELOW

Up there there's nothing,
Down here there's everything,
Down below there's even . . .

It all started when I found myself
Floating down, down and down,
In somewhat shock was I dreaming?
I landed on the sea bed,
And lay for hours helpless,
The sea was very calm,
Everything started to glitter,
They came closer and closer around me,
There were millions of little seahorses,
They stuck around my body,
Curling their tails to every part.
They looked at me through the corners
Of their eyes, smiles on their faces,
And lifted me as if almost I . . .
Could fly,
And landed me safely on a shore,
As if in a dream,
It seems that they saved me,
Down below there's even seahorses.

A Bhambra

A FLIGHT OF FANCY

The sun shone in a clear blue sky
a light breeze brushing the tops
of dandelions blowing white puffs
of seed into the air, scattering them
far and wide.

A mixture of buttercups and daisies
as far as the eye can see
so peaceful bar the sheep bleating
in the field below.

Soon we were flying above the
tall pines clustered together
forming dark cushions on fields
of coloured carpets.

We soared across the sky towards
the sea glittering there in the
sun, tiny boats bobbing up and down
in the wake of ships heading for the isles,
so quiet and serene.

Can they see us, do they wish they
could be on high, flying like a bird
in this glorious blue sky?

Soft clouds are forming up ahead
To shade us from the sun
Some shaped with heads like horses
Galloping off into the beyond
Followed by chariots in their wake.

Soon we will be returning
To our field of wild flowers
Dusk casting shadows from the
Trees below, the Condor comes
Home to rest.

Beryl Smyter

MARILYN MONROE

This is the story of Marilyn Monroe
A child who had far to go
So much sadness, so much strife
She did not have a happy life
Her mother in a mental home
Which left her lots of time to roam
Foster parents who only wanted the money
Not a life of milk and honey
At twelve she lost her virginity
Was abused and scarred with impunity
Then one day she got her chance
And into films she did advance
Her charm and beauty in great demand
She soon became Queen of Hollywood Land
But she was too naive, found no true friend
And for herself she had to fend
She was betrayed by many men
But for true love she had a yen
But men only sought themselves to please
From her body their pleasure to seize
In the end betrayed by all
She took the final curtain call
Did she die by her own hand
Or was it some dark secret planned?
And now the years gone by we'll never know
What happened to the beautiful sad Monroe.

June Clare

A WINTER'S TALE

The lines were down
There wasn't a sound
As lightning tore the sky
Flashing wires alive with light
Illuminating darkness, sparks flying high
Snow fell deep throughout the blustery night
Posts like soldiers fell to the ground
Whilst snowflakes covered all around
Marooned on a hill I ventured out in the light
Confronted with a spectacular sight
A crocheted web of branches
Layered with snow
Trees covered in white lace
Until the silken strands of sun laid them bare again
The snow disappears without a trace
In the winter of eighty-four
The land was transformed
Then defrosted and left as before.

Jenny Anderson

LOVE IN THE SEASONS

We fell in love in the spring,
when daffodils carpet the ground
with a fragrance that lingers.
Young trees find their feet,
pointing skywards, with eager fingers.

By summer, love had blossomed,
our whole life was filled with magic.
The air was heavy with the scent
of honeysuckle and roses.
In passion only, our time was spent.

In autumn, out lives were still golden.
But as the last leaves finally fell,
the intensity was slipping away.
The enchantment in each other was fading,
no magical feeling would stay.

By winter the landscapes
were transformed to a dazzle of white.
Trees looked naked and old.
A hushed stillness hung in the air;
and our love had grown empty and cold.

Anne Palmer

WHEN SUMMER FADES

When summer days are gone - once more,
With evening darkness appears - ever more;
Then I'll take a walk down Childhood Lane
There to browse and laugh once again.
All my old chums will really be old by now,
Wonder what they are like, what they do!
As I wander down that long winding lane
I'm only dreaming until summer comes again.
But as I wander at least I laugh and smile,
For childhood days were the golden ones of life.
My thoughts journey on to many happy holidays,
Mostly taken by the sea, memories that flood back to me,
As I dine and partake another glass of choice wine
I'll ponder slowly along that very long lane;
From my childhood days - to holidays by the sea
Then again to explore many photographs old and new
With family and friends - winter can be cosy,
You see for it won't seem very long like this,
Before - spring will guide back summer again.

Des Lamb

FLORENCE'S POTTERY CLASSES

Florence went to evening classes
Though well beyond the learning age
Never a thought of what to do
Pottery the passion took centre stage

Vases fluted and slim she made
Green and grey glaze she used
Plates with dragons now a vase too
Not perfect on which a dragon is fused

Nothing to Florence was impossible
Everything in clay has to be tried
Her Clumber spaniel called Rudi
Replaced in clay (he was run over and died)

Such a loss to a lonesome widow
That dog was her companion and joy
His pot effigy was rather unbalanced
But pink pot painted white was her boy

One owl joined the other made of concrete
This group kept guard on the porch step
Since then Florence has gone to join Rudi
Left her pots to me I've no porch just a step

Jennifer A Major

THE WALL

Here adorning the slim neck of Britannia
Hadrian hung his chain of command
the wild north winds were untameable
a mighty empire glared from the skyline

From east to west through centuries spent
silent against the savagery of time
an iron realm had passed into antiquity
now modern man stands emperor

Gateway of the gods coursing the whinsill
long ransacked and abandoned alone
mere stubble upon the high rocky crags
still these Saxon eyes bare flesh to its bones

How I love to accompany such noble stones
and breathe in the ancient air
following the distant echoes of Latin tongues
a special place to dream

Gerard Wilson

A HORSEY TALE

Sylvia said to Maurice, 'I know just what we'll do'
'I'll take you to try something, that I know is new to you
So off to the riding school they went, to find a friendly horse
Sylvia took the lead, Maurice needed gentle force

Sylvia mounted up and cantered off on her ride
A 7ft stallion then appeared, Maurice's eyes opened wide
'Come on' the stable-hand coaxed 'he's as gentle as can be'
'How do I get on it?' Maurice asked 'Will it get down on its knees?'

A pair of steps were provided so Maurice climbed on board
He held the reigns carefully, so not to scare the horse
A slap upon its rear and it began to trot
Our hero's face turned quite white and his stomach into a knot

All went so well until the horse, stopped beside a pool
Maurice hung on for dear life, feeling such a fool
'Yank his bridle' came a shout 'he'll know just what to do'
Said Maurice 'If he wants a drink, it's nothing to do with you'

After what seemed forever the horse made his way back home
Maurice alighted thankfully, his legs were not his own
Sylvia returned full of smiles her ride had been a delight
Maurice said 'Never, never again, next time I'll take my bike'

Gillian Mullett

THE REWARD

Watch your children grow
And help them sow
The seeds of life,
Hoping life will be sweet
Not full of strife
And deceit.
Do your very best
Then the rest
They will sort out
One way or another
And, though they sometimes doubt
The words of a mother,
They will make their own way,
Then you will hear them say
'Thanks Mum.'
To have their love
Is worth all the worry,
This is the reward
You will never be sorry.

M S Reid

A CRYING GAME

I made one promise, I was never to cry
and if I did, he was never to see.
Then I doubled that promise for others,
if you're going to cry, don't come.

I told my mum. We had to be strong.
Positive only, I guess I was semi-impressed.
Her eyes were all red and swollen when she arrived.
But at this stage I don't think he knew his own name.

She did not cry in front of him
and neither did his sisters.
I cried twice.
First, when they said they could cure him.

He remained so strong.
Only nine years old
facing what many adults never have to.
Just once he gave in and so did I, behind his back.

Maria Bernadette Potter

UNEXPECTED

You came quite unexpected
A bundle full of woe
Creating quite a problem
And an all time low.

But time was on your side it seems
How could one not resist
The smiling eyes, the toothless grin
And waving chubby fist.

Times were hard - can't be denied
For baby needs cost money
But love and caring is for free
We'd found the milk and honey.

You came quite unexpected
But brought with you such wealth
Look forward to the times ahead
Love, happiness and health.

Margarette L Damsell

BLANK EXPRESSIONS

Feeling sad without a reason
Not knowing why or anything.
Feeling bad, lost in confusion
Mind's a blank, no thoughts at all.
No emotions or revelations
No memories or tides to turn.
Just a blank sheet of paper
Sad feelings come tumbling.
On the outside looking inward
Isolation starts to set in.
A crowded room, yet on a desert
As if in a room alone.
No expressions, no emotions
Eyes blank, gazing into space.
Trying to piece together
Feelings that you can't explain.
Bodies cold; yet hot with sweat
Nothing seems, as it should be.
Wanting to sleep, without being sleepy
Tell me what is happening.

A M Williamson

ON THE ROAD

Clip-clop of hooves. My mind's alerted.
Gypsies pass, their eyes averted.
Painted, bright wagons in rainbow colours,
Drawn by four tired horses.

A black, a bay, two piebalds, led
By a man who strode ahead.
With him a boy, his jersey red.
In their wake a woman follows
Clip-clop of hooves.

Pale pink skirt, her blue blouse faded,
The woman and her girl undaunted.
Primeval instinct? Nature lovers?
A longing in me? I have no answers.
Now passed from view and only the echoed
Clip-clop of hooves.

Isobel G King

WISEGUYS

Sicilian eh?
The country of hot cracks in the road
Filled with the cement of bones
Lupare torn
Lawfully born
Omerta alone

The heat of cassetta and crows
Jackets over power and love
Cosa
La nostra above
And weakness of the dove
Wiseguys
All talking God

The meaning of bred
Where once there stood
A justice inbred
A man on the throne
To the mountains was shown
Guilano once said
While the living still grow
All those who betray me
Are dead

Anora Kay

EL POZO

I went to Altafulla. I had been there once before
And seen a tiny restaurant whose sign above the door
Read simply, 'El Pozo' a name which cast a spell on me -
A haunting fascination luring me with urgency.

Its ancient door concealed a cave of stone and charm inside,
Beneath historic arches were the tables laid with pride,
And all with Spanish influence - no tourists to be seen.
Whilst dining, a harpist appeared - he was an Argentine.

He played with such magnificence - there was no spoken word,
His music so exquisite, no better could be heard,
With fervour and with feeling, with passion and with calm,
He played his harp expressing all his music's special charm.

Astounded diners sat transfixed in awe, enraptured there,
Spellbound in silent wonder, captivated by the air.
All knowledge of the time was lost, he played, no pause for rest
Till finally, we all arose, applauding him with zest.

We'd heard a master of his art. One thing I surely know,
Next time I find myself in Spain, I'm back in El Pozo,
For there's a buried treasure with such talent rarely shown,
Deep down in Altafulla where a jewel shines in stone.

Joy Saunders

TOPICS, THOUGHTS, THEMES

A scene, flower, times to convey
Description, meditation in verse,
May arouse, provoke or replay
Topics, thoughts, themes to focus.

Sad, glad, memorable moments
Moving poets to pen deep, rich rhyme
Readers remember if cadent
Topics, thoughts, themes quite sublime.

Rhythm and rhyme is harmony
Lyrics simple to read and recall
Orchestrated in symphony
Topics, thoughts, themes to enthral.

Nursery rhymes to epitaphs,
We learn to read and write balladry,
In midst may bring tears, chuckling laugh
To topics, thoughts, themed poetry.

Hilary Jill Robson

SADNESS TO GLADNESS

I saw a girl who had sadness in her eyes
But I had gladness in mine . . . I was lucky
My face was happy but her face was sad
I told her my name
She told me hers

I told her my story which was happy and glad
She told me hers which was *awful* and *sad*
She shared all her troubles
'Bout bullies and fear
I wanted to help her though I shed a tear

So we decided to go straight to tell
At our earliest chance which was after the bell.
Our teacher was kindly and helpful and sweet
And my friend felt much better and said she could now eat

Our problem was over as the bully was caught
And a very strong lesson the bully was taught
So let it be noted that whenever in fear
If you're bullied just report it
And do away with the tears!

Rochelle Peltier

MY EVENING WITH OTIS REDDING

Fresh from the shower with lather abounding,
now rinsed off with skin squeaky clean.
Then lashings of lotion absorbed by my skin
to maintain both its softness and sheen.
A dab here with perfume, a dab there for luck
then a dab just in case you don't notice.
Now a freshly washed bathrobe around me I tuck
as I start to prepare for my evening with Otis.
So subtle the make-up applied with such care
for I know without doubt that my love will be there.
Then I gently comb back and tuck in my long hair
for I'm now fully dressed and know others will stare.
As I make my way down to the place that he's waiting
so sure he'll adore the effort I'm making.
Our eyes lock, he's singing his love for me there
on the TV as I sit, now he's mine for the taking.
Alright so I'm foolish, but I know he can see
through the screen at me sitting with feet under knee.
It's that voice, I just melt as he sings out to me
and I'm happy to be just where I want to be.

Channon Cornwallis

GO TO BED

I do not want to go to bed
Because of the nightmares
I need to talk to someone yes,
Someone who really cares.

I do not want to go to bed
Because my mind is all mixed up
Even at three in the morning
It has still not had enough.

I do not want to go to bed
Because I will toss and turn all night
Please, please help me somehow
From starting another fight.

Keith L Powell

HIS DREAM

His hand shook as he wrote the words
He had dreamt of him again
Rising from the ashes in a cloud of dust,
Sweeping the years from his brow.
The earth had quivered and quaked
And cracked in two:
Revealing another world beyond man.
Feathers had enclouded the air as
Thick as mist on a lake as he rose.
Birds had screamed as the air grew thick,
Smoke seeped from the ground;
Leaves burned as the fire grew,
Humanity drowned in the lake.

The pencil fell from his hands
As he remembered the appalling face.
Dark visions brought on by night,
Darkness enclosing his mind.
The eyes so dark, yet so bright
Burned a hole into his soul.
He could still smell the burning earth
And hear the crying souls.
An oppressive weight quashed him
As the shadow of his dream surrounded him;
A scream was the last sound to be heard,
In the apocalypse of one disciple.

Sandra MacLean

Day To Remember, 19th August 2000

Day to remember, 19th August 2000
A day to be remembered
I gave birth to my baby boy
I was induced early
In labour for hours I was
Oh when is my baby coming I thought
Push, push, push
I had an epidural
I then rested awhile, fell asleep
Then I was awake
The midwife said,
'I can see baby's head, push.'
I did, baby came out
Yes my little baby boy
My angel, bundle of joy
How unbelievable, me, Michelle Knight
A mother, how fantastic
I called my baby boy
Michael Apollo Ronan Chakotay Knight
He was born on
Saturday 19th August 2000
My millennium boy.

Michelle Knight

Rhys

Through floods of desolation,
while gnats sucked at our blood,
with grim determination
we fought the clutching mud.

Persisting despite deep wounds,
resisting those of greed
enamoured, we sought the boon
of love's blossoming seed.

Then, when the future seemed dim,
arrived lucidity -
Miracle Rhys, the next limb
of our family tree.

Perry McDaid

ANNIVERSARY REFLECTIONS (THE RAKE'S PROGRESS)

Our Eric's the lad who liked to have fun,
Out with mates camping, with Bonner and gun.
School days passed and workhouse began,
Skiving and Whitleys were part of the plan.
Rover scouting together on summer night hikes,
Then good friends touring on their motorbikes.

Our Eric grew handsome, tall, debonair,
He often went dancing with scarcely a care.
Then along came sweet Judith - a filly with charm,
Poor Eric was smitten, folks warned him of harm.
Too late he reflected after taking the pledge,
What looked good to him, was the end of the wedge.

With bills and debts Eric's troubles began,
And all too soon he was pushing a pram.
Not one but two, his load multiplied,
'You'll have to work harder,' poor Judith sighed.
Washing dishes, gardening and house painting too,
Life was a drag, with too much to do.

The hard years together now dim in the past,
It's obvious too that their good times still last.
After 25 years their love still burns bright,
To Eric his Judith's pure gold in his sight.
So onwards together they walk hand in hand,
With pride friends declare, 'They're the best in the land!'

Roger F Jamieson

LADYHAWK

I found you by chance
Whilst walking over the moor,
Your wing broken, your body punctured,
You were just a tiny chick.
I took you home and nursed you back to health,
Your wounds not allowing you back into the wild.
Years have gone by, you have brought so much joy.
Every morning we fly the moor.
The bracken crunches under my boots,
Sunshine breaks over the tors
Enhancing the peace and tranquillity
To the open spaces which are everlasting.
You're excited, you squawk, bells ring around your feet,
With hood removed, you fake your flight
Then you take to the sky,
Gliding in sheer elegance.
With riveting speed you catch your treat
But on the ground you look for me with all your trust
Knowing I won't allow you to come to any harm.
You are my ladyhawk.

Angie

PELICAN CITY

Like delegates they congregate
Important business to relate,
Between each flight they take a break
Wining and dining, east of the Lake

No litter, boats, or fishing line
A nesting area - this place is fine,
The geese and harriers try to invade:
Pelicans stare, they hide in the shade

The Avian convention of the wetland.
Performed by an elegant Pelican band:
Declaring the area, an aviary or rest
'Pelican City' with a five-star crest.

Fay Bullock

A SEASIDE VISIT

The children set out with their parents one day
To go to the seaside, where they could play
Together on the sands with their bucket and spade,
Away from the traffic - their day would be made.
Both parents could relax and have no fear
As the children made sandcastles - so very near.
But after a while they relaxed too well,
And the children wandered off after a spell -
Being tired of the sand, wanting something new,
A different game - as all children do.
But of course very soon children lose their way
And further into difficulty they stray!
On rousing the mother looked where the children should be,
The castles were there but no child could she see.
Hurriedly she explained to the man at her side,
Who at once stood up, searching far and wide
Among the crowded beach that day,
Where plenty of other children were hard at play.
After a while he saw with delight
His own two children, in sorry plight,
Comforting each other, as hand in hand they stood,
Looking for Mummy and Daddy as best they could.
How their faces lit up when Daddy they saw,
Jumping into his arms, secure once more.
The parents and children all shed many tears
As they were united once more - no more fears!

Jean C Pease

RINSEY HEAD

The sea's speech slurs silvery in the settling sun
hovering like a huge hawk over the drowning horizon.

We come upon fallen towers at catastrophe's edge,
a solitary house hanging its tapestry on a clifftop's ledge

supervising the monumental operations of the waves
washing down the lunar hollows of craggy caves.

Yachts perch on the blue-grey panorama of the Atlantic Ocean,
sails scribbling strange alphabets on our virgin vision.

Yesterday's buzzard's gone, the skylark's celebration
echoes in our singing blood, our heart's inundation

flooding home with our wheeling walk and humming hedges
alive as the sense of love overflowing our life's beaches.

Returning, ten year olds cry like toddlers in the car park,
their scarlet mother praying for the swift descent of the dark.

Roland Gurney

THE BASKET RUN

With wire basket hanging from left hand
And only sixty seconds it to fill
We rushed to grab the things that we had planned,
Then took it to the lady at the till.

We'd chocolate and envelopes and books
Whilst some sought coffee, tea and other goods;
We took from shelves and also off the hooks
Both paper items and a lot of food.

But as we rushed to choose our hearts' desire
Much cash was gained for children on the streets,
So as we sit this winter by the fire
We'll know we've helped them as we eat our sweets.

M S Whale

THREE PILGRIMAGES

To Walsingham they came
Pilgrims of old
Poor, rich, sick,
Religious from far and wide,
Kings with crown and jewels
From Slipper Chapel processing
Barefoot with humble mien
To the Virgin's shrine.

To Walsingham we came
With pilgrims of every sphere
In this two thousand Holy Year,
People of more sophistication
In luxurious coach and car,
Few barefoot, yet sincere,
United in faith with men of old.

To Walsingham they came
Travelling from afar
Swallows gracefully gliding in
Twittering to the rafters
Joining in with rapturous song
Hosannas with our pilgrim throng:
Nature and man united.

Patricia Weitz

REQUEST

Love me not because you must,
Out of loyalty of trust.
Love not just for my sake,
Because of blunder a mistake.

Love me like oceans deep,
Into my inner soul to creep.
A substance that will solidify,
My soul my heart will satisfy.

The constant hunger, endless yearning,
The search for love, not underling.
Such love to find I know not where,
Yet hope within is always there.

If your love be what I seek,
Will lift me up to mountain peak.
If your love will end my quest,
Will bring salvation, eternal rest.

Then to you I say with simplicity,
Offer me such love with sincerity.
And I await to gratify,
Such solid love to satisfy.

Shula Bailey

THE LETTER

It came this morning,
Smelling of musty earth.
The smell of the trenches.

He didn't say much.
Not even where he was,
Except in France somewhere.

He said he loved and missed me
That the war would soon be over
And he'd be coming home.

I read it this morning,
Words blurred and smudged with tears,
For yesterday I learned that he'd died.

Joyce Walker

AGATHA

I don't know if it was a dream but,
Beyond my memory I do recall this place
Standing in the bay the murky salt water
Lapped by her feet, the cold strange mists
Rising from the depth.
Standing still 'in trance'
Listening to its murmuring voice,
Yes! A recurrent dream,
Or so it seems.
I know they will be seeking me but,
I cannot leave here, not yet,
I cannot leave and just forget.
'Who are you?' spake a young man
On a sandy mound thereby,
'*Agatha.* I am sixteen' she did reply.
And' I!
Live in Greengates, yonder it lies.
He looked 'But that place is derelict,'
He turned his head,
'I must go home' she said.
You jest me,
Within the mists he barely saw 'Agatha' sink -
slowly beneath the sea.

Agnes Burns Lawson

THE NURSE

She works so diligently
Day and night,
Her caring hands soothe many a fevered brow.
Her ward sister never gives her a row -
She is so good and faithful in her job.
From no patient, or poor person would she rob.
Honest, loyal as the day is long -
Never doing a bit of wrong.
She writes the chart day and night.
She has saved many from an awful fright.
They never fear the operation chair -
When they are in her loving care.
They sleep so well all night long.
And often hear her cheerful song!
She goes 'off-duty' early in the morning.
Then, without warning, the day is dawning!
As she leaves the hospital, all the patients there:
Thank the Lord and feel full of good cheer.

Shane V Simons

COUNTRYSIDE ARTIST

Painting a beautiful countryside scene,
perched above grass, lush and green.
Attempting to convey to others,
peace and tranquillity.
Like being in bed,
on a cold winter's night,
all wrapped up in covers.

Countryside artist sits, absorbing all around,
inspired, with the wild countryside sound.
Echoing its voice into interpretative art,
creating visions for people, living far apart.
From the freedom of an open space,
countryside artists, so clearly find,
waiting, right in front of their face.

How inspiring they are.

Andy Monnacle

APPLES

God walked in Eden's garden, lent to Adam and to Eve,
And noticed that their fig leaves weren't in place,
But when young Adam saw his God displeased with what he'd done,
His colour turned bright red all round his face!

'Don't look like that,' he said to God, 'I can explain it all -
'Twas just a kiss, you see, not what you think' -
'Oh well,' said God, 'if that's the truth, what made your face go red?
When I made you, I only used the pink!'

'You can't fool me,' God said to him, 'that Satan's been in here
And you've been eating apples, I can see,
And though I told you both to leave the fruit just where it was,
You've both been eating apples off my tree!'

'No, no!' they said, that guilty pair, 'we kissed but nothing else,
Although we will admit our passion soars;'
'If that's the case,' God said to them, 'explain why is it then
Just by your feet, I see two apple cores?'

God moves in a mysterious way,
He knows if we're just kissing;
He calls it 'sin', if, when we stray,
He finds two apples missing!

S R Eveson

THE STICKLEBACK

A stickleback,
Three-spined
And red-breasted,
Is trapped
In the jam jar
By small boys.
He's bumping at,
He raps at
The jam jar glass.
His red breast
And his three spines
Need to go
Back into the
Cool, dark pond.

Kaye Axon

UNTITLED

Any port in a storm
It's nice to have a friend.
Any port in a storm
Someone to depend
Any port in a storm
Faithful until the end
Any port in a storm
Goodbye my dearest friend.

P Allen

MOOR PONIES

Born free that's for sure,
Free to race across the moor.
In the gorse we can hide,
On the wind we seem to ride.
We toss our heads up high,
Trying to reach the stars in the sky.
Soft ground hides the thunder of our hooves,
Prints in the earth are our proof.
Proof to where we could be found,
By the marks left in the ground.
We love the wind tugging our mane,
Some of us they've tried to tame.
They watch that we come to no harm,
Winter we're fetched near to a farm.
Feed us hay when grass is full of frost,
And make sure none of us are lost.
Not many people do we trust,
But in winter we know we must.

Margaret Upson

LOVE AND DEATH
(Dedicated to my late wife)

We stood side by side and exchanged rings and a vow,
I loved you then as much as I love you now.
Ten months later I prayed for you, to live my life for you
I would gladly give now once more dressed as my bride.
As I gave you that final kiss the heart inside me died
And through God's mercy you're now free from pain.
Wait for me Linda, we will meet again.

Philip Wright

SPOTS ON YOUR TONGUE

There's a little boy in my class
With spots on his tongue
He gets them quite a lot you know
Even though he's very young
He's forever telling stories
Which are sometimes quite untrue
And I'm afraid he'll pass them on
Perhaps to me or you
So I think I'd better tell him
It's much nicer to sing a song
Instead of telling stories
And getting spots on his tongue.

S A Ward

WALLACE HARTLEY

Wallace Hartley from Colne Lancashire
He died on the Titanic
Go and see his memorial
He worked on the ship

His call to play the last hymn
Will always be known

Now in deep silence
TV shows us crusted shapes,
We recall the dead.

Mavis Catlow

A QUIET STORM

Hands reaching out to hold the world,

In kindness, warmth, support and in strength,

Holding firmly, yet gently, each precious life strand,

Supporting one another over life's treasured plan,

Uplifting, unyielding, towards a much promised land,

Never bending or unbroken, though never quite spoken,

Clasped tightly together to help weather the storms,

Leading us back safely through the embrace of his arms.

Katherine Quaye

THREADS OF MY DREAMS

As I daydream of the early summer's grass
and yellow irises that grow by a lake en mass
I know that no one can follow when I dream
or tell me what my dreams might mean
I am the one who weaves my dreams
I am the thread that makes the seams
I spin the memories where they begin and end
Will the river be wild, will I reach its bend?
But my favourite dream is of a hot summer day
and a quiet gentle river where baby otters play
and ancient trees give shade from the sun's heat
and the earth is cool beneath my hot bare feet.

Maureen Cassidy

STRANGE LOOK

A wasps nest in the garden
Brought shivers down my spine
I donned some special clothing
No flesh to see or find
With brush in hand I clobbered it
And thought now you take that
But several minutes later found
They'd just flown back
This time I thought of water
And almost made a pond
The hole inside the hose pipe
Was letting water on the ground
The postman brought a parcel
He looked a little strange
For one thing I'd forgotten
I had a lace curtain around my red face.

M Rossi

JACK THE CAT - DIAMONDS ARE FOREVER

He has diamonds all over his paws,
I saw them
quite distinctly
When he came in from the rain,
stretching and grooming,
Catching the sunlight
through his fur
While I stroked his preciousness.
for that moment . . .

Margarette Phillips

TIME

Time that will always be one step ahead
that will not wait around no matter how unprepared
we may be for events that were hurriedly planned
time won't slow down nor will it understand
how important it is that we don't arrive late
for a prearranged meeting or perhaps for a date
clocks will carry on ticking as the hands move around
going from minutes to hours making barely a sound
even now so unnoticed the present becomes past
it is gone and we realise that the present never lasts
as progression continues and the future passes by
do we ever stop to wonder or to look for reasons why
so much time is wasted either lost or wished away
when instead we should be making the most of every day

Helen King

ALONE WITH MY THOUGHTS

I sit alone upon my seat,
to the sound of crashing waves,
and to my left, in the mist,
there lies a lonely grave,
and within the grave,
there sleeps a man,
at peace within the field,
but not alone as believed
for at his feet another,
upon which lies a lovely sight,
one lead and one collar,
friends in life for all to see
God bless forever and ever.

M J Wallis

INTERVAL

Awoke desiring still more music making
differently though now to last night
then the more laid back slow movement called
but now eager, vibrant, insistent
mutually the beat's rhythm dictates
demanding the fast flowing movement
agonisingly dissonant
we collide though in the recapitulation
richly flowing timbres caressing mutually
resolving into the major key
wonderfully freeing and liberating.

We lie back content
knowing eternity
the tiny moment between movements
satisfying until the tide returns.

Robert D Shooter

LISA-MARIE

My dearest Lisa-Marie,
You mean the whole world to me.
I waited so long for you, you see
I thought you never ever would be
My sweet little baby girl
You have changed my life around
And left me all in a whirl
Your cute little fingers and toes
A beautiful smile, a small button nose
You grow more lovely every day
My dear Lisa-Marie, what more can I say
To me you are a dream come true
My darling daughter, I dearly love you.

Trudie Sullivan

NEW LIFE

When an erupting volcano jets
Lava and fire, a molten sea
Relentlessly advances and covers
Everywhere heedless of feasts, villages, orchards.
All is changed into smouldering ruins.
Children, men and beasts,
Frozen in their last act of running away,
Are still what they were,
Caught forever in the same cindery grave.
When the volcano bellows
'Forgive me' and grumbles himself to sleep
Men and women count their losses,
Bury their dead and build again
Their lives until the earth will tremble again.

A Matheson

DREAM A DREAM

I dreamt
Oh so long ago.
A dream
Came true
It was you
I'll treasure always
From above
That special love.
I dreamed of long ago.
Given to me for a short time
Here on this Earth below.
What a dream
I was allowed to know.

Anne Macleod

SCENE OF ACCIDENT

To look at an accident
And see the empty trolley
Waiting for the person
Trapped in the car.

To see the person
Laying, not knowing
What they are going through inside.
What injuries, what upheaval it causes.

How the person feels
After the car plunges down a ditch.
What panic, what pain, what anguish.

To be taken to hospital.
Faced with uncertainty
As to what is happening,
Now knowing.

No one knows,
But God knows and cares.
He cares about us all
Because He loves us.

Julie Smith

SILVER TREES

Hesitant, I asked if I might take him home.
He thanked me. Could not have realised
The pleasure his assent had given me
For I had long felt drawn towards
His solitariness.

He said: 'There is my house,
Its garden sadly overgrown.
See the tall birches?
When first we came
We called our home Silver Trees.'

They are much taller now.
His wife had died long since.
His hair is white
As the stick he must carry
To guide his way.

But on entering the gate
I saw him raise his arm as in
Acknowledgement of their constancy
And, looking back,
I saw a rainbow arching

Above the Silver Trees.

Louise Rogers

SHEP

We had our dear Shep, he was just six weeks old
So lovely and gentle and cuddly to hold
When we went to choose him, he came wagging his tail
He was born in a village in the Severn Vale

He soon settled down with Snowie the rabbit
To play on the lawn was a regular habit
Newborn chickens with the mother hen
He guarded them gently, when out of their pen

Shep was very obedient and anxious to please
He was blessed with good health, hardly any vet fees
Chasing round our large garden, he would bark at the planes
Kept him fit as a fiddle with walks down the lanes

Each afternoon about quarter to four
Shep would lie down, on the drive by the door
Awaiting the children to come home from the school
He liked bacon and ham and drinks that were cool

Our Blue Merle Sheltie we had seventeen years
He was partially blind and went deaf in the ears
That night at the vets, with a tear in our eye
We held him and stroked him as we said goodbye.

T Rutherford

FOOD FOR THOUGHT

Sitting at hotel table family had enormous shock.
At next table sat a lady weighing such a lot.
Gentleman sat by her so was thought by us,
He'd restrict her food intake should she make a fuss.
But no; with big plate to starters food went she,
Took melon, avocado, roll mops, salad and pate.
We looked at each other, thinking if that is her diet,
It really, wasn't working; we weren't going to try it.
Waiter then brought roast meat, vegetables as well,
Extra rolls she'd ask for, no wonder she looked *swell.*
Maybe it was bad manners watching he and she,
But our eyes did not believe what went in that lady.
Through though yet she was *not* as for her dessert course
She filled two plates up fast, showing no remorse,
Chocolate mousse, strawberry cheesecake, salad of mixed berry,
Fresh fruit salad, creamed apple crumble followed on you see.
She cannot eat more we all felt, were all wrong on that score,
When she had her coffee ate entire plate of petit fours
All of us sat speechless till my son said brokenly,
Pity groom to carry her over threshold *and* turn key.
She sat there looking as if was, heaven's keys she'd bought,
How she consumed and kept it down we all find
> *food for thought.*

Barbara Goode

FOR LANI

I recall the day my beautiful dog became ill
Unable to walk, she lay so still
A stroke had left her unable to stand
She *knew* my intentions as I laid my hands . . .
Upon her body.
For two weeks at least, she lay on her bed
I cannot recall, how many tears I shed
But *her* willingness and courage
And my determination was *strong*
These two put together, helped her along.
The vet had said there was nothing to be done
But *she* was my baby, I was her mum
And so I soldiered on, though others could not see
Don't you worry girl, I *will* have you on your feet.
Eventually it happened, one day out of the blue
The joy of seeing her walk was overwhelming
I can tell you
For it was only through *faith* - hers *and* mine
That we managed to cross over, that final line
She stayed by my side, for quite some time.
But although *now* she has gone
And her body again 'whole'
She will always stay deep within my soul.

Sam Williams

BB The Poison Pixie

Watch out for this small character, he's evil but he's bright,
Many folk have learned to loathe this very toxic sprite.
His features are all normal to any fleeting glance,
He'll lure you to within his trust, then on your grave will dance.

BB is short for bumblebee, but never makes no honey,
Stinging you when you least expect, he's only after money.
Going to untold measures of deception and disguise,
Stooping to the lowest depths lifting coins from dead men's eyes.

Being somewhat vertically challenged he stands small on his pegs,
Inserting heel lifts in his shoes to try extend his legs.
But plastic surgery's marvellous his pointed ears don't show
And wearing normal fashioned shoes after straightened curly toes.

This pixie has a small forked tongue which spits so many lies,
With venom like a rattlesnake, deceptive for his size.
So you may have gathered conscience he has none,
Corrupting minds of anyone to make sure that he's won.

A nasty little elf he is, playing on your greatest fears,
Would take the breath from sleeping babes, then say it was your idea.
Watch out for his allies known as the 'brownie boys'
Following close behind him, he used them like toys.

Some people are quite fortunate and only poisoned slight
Escaping from his evil words can still tell wrong from right.
The way to beat him is so clear to flush out all his lies,
Just tell the truth it makes him cringe and cuts him back to size.

Jim Fraser

THE FLOOD

Joe's class had been busy painting,
There was colour and mess everywhere.
Lucy had blue streaks on her nose,
Simon had red in his hair.

Their paintings were really good though,
The colours were bright and gay.
'If you've finished, go and wash, please,'
They heard Mrs Barker say.

When Joe went down to the cloakroom,
He couldn't believe what he saw:
Three boys from his class were filling the sinks,
There was water all over the floor.

They shouted and giggled and stamped about,
Their voices were really loud.
They splashed each other and everyone else,
They were drawing quite a crowd.

Later, when it was playtime,
Outside the staffroom door,
With dirty, tear-stained faces,
The three boys sat on the floor.

Mrs Barker had caught them red-handed,
She'd really been after their blood.
So, as well as missing their playtime,
She'd made them clear up the flood!

Sue Smith

TABBY CAT

One day when I came home from work
I saw a small cat on the drive;
he stared at me with frightened eyes,
fur flattened, only half alive.

I made no movement, but I smiled,
and he gazed back, then turned and ran.
From that day on I watched for him,
our friendship, in this way, began.

He came next to the kitchen door,
where I had left a bowl of milk;
he started taking food and drink,
and he filled out, his fur like silk.

Soon was he sitting on my knee,
and then he slept upon our bed.
He was a handsome tabby cat,
with pure green eyes, and noble head.

He was the king of all the house,
the garden, too, was his domain.
He made friends with the other cats,
to all extended his mild reign.

Then, we were glad we took him in,
When poor and broken, weak and thin.

Patricia Marston

PER ARDUA - 'AD' ERNIA

They took me from the City Hall
And put me in the RAF,
They gave me bromide in my tea
And a haircut that was naff.

They put me in a Nissen hut
And made me shine the floor,
They made me wash my knife and fork
Outside the cookhouse door,

They taught me how to shoot a gun,
They taught me how to drill,
They sent me out to bivouac
Upon a lonely hill,

They let me loose in Bridgnorth town,
I chased the girls with glee,
And when I caught 'em, soon forgot
The bromide in my tea!

On leave I swore I'd killed the Hun,
Huge men who looked like Satan,
I told of war and pestilence
Not bad for Market Drayton!

Farewell the RAF, I'm back here in
The City Hall again,
There's only one regret I have -
I never saw a plane!

Peter Davies

THE LITTLE SWEEP

'Tis a gruesome tale I tell
A little orphan's life of hell
Many a mother stops to weep
At the monument to the little sweep

Apprenticed at the age of ten
To a Mr Davis - known as Ben
From some parish workhouse taken
A little chimney sweep in the makin'

Valentine Gray's post had begun
October eighteen twenty-one
But by the turn of twenty-two
The little sweeps short life was thro'

Winter was so grim and hard
His washroom was a cold backyard
All bruised and beaten and ill-used
By cruel master so abused

The attic high - his little room
Looked out on graveyard - oh, what gloom!
It seemed to beckon 'Be my guest'
In three short months he took his rest

No gravestones now - 'tis a park today
Just one fine stone - reads Valentine Gray
'Tis good to know the Lord doth keep
Care of the little angel sweep.

Norah Page

MY LIFE TELLS A STORY

For I walk the path of life
I suffered pain
I have accomplished my dreams.
My mother died when I was nine
My life changed but not for the worse
For travelling was now my gain
From Nevis shores
To the Virgin Isles
My life took a course unknown.
New friends were made
New schools entertained
School yard drama
Brought folks from far and near
When my bullies received a shock
And one was left frothing from the mouth
Sirens cars filled the yard
But there was no punishment for me
For the bullies were warned each day
This day my body mechanism had to fight for me.
Life have so much in store for me
That's why England called for me
America, Jamaica, Barbados and others
Are countries I have toured
For my spirits are free so I just have to roam.

Carolie Pemberton

A MAGICAL MOMENT

A unique glittering moment most precious and rare,
A brilliant holiday memory that you once did share,
A surprise thoughtful gift, that gave great joy,
A bunch of colourful flowers or a longed-for toy.
A camera's very lucky well-timed and focused click
A baby's innocent captivating smile snapped real quick.
A lover's passionate kiss, so thrilling so terrific,
A little egg cracks and opens and out pops a chick.
A congratulatory, exciting and an unbelievable *win,*
A shock, you are speechless, head goes into a spin!
A letter or unexpected parcel, a tantalising surprise
A leaping heart suddenly soars up into the skies
A day comes, blends into the night, then a brand new dawn,
A mysterious magical miracle of brightness, light is born!
A wonderful peace, as many sleep, surrounds all each morn,
A silent sunrise appears and the sky will brilliantly adorn.
A new awakening as birds everywhere greet the dawn and sing,
A dawn chorus is inspiring and a momentous magical thing,
A bird-song is of thanks to their maker and their king,
A heavenly moment of bliss envelops and surrounds everything.
A few tiny raindrops freshen plants and pretty flowers kiss
A sleepy head slumbers on, alas these moments will miss.
A challenge I give, to one and all each bright new day
A thought, a gift, a *magical moment* could make someone's day.

Stella Bush-Payne

CHILDHOOD MEMORIES

When I was young, I liked to play,
I liked to play outdoors everyday,
I had a tent in my back green
And often dressed up as a gala queen.
We put on shows for all the kids,
Whatever was the latest TV quiz.
We played peevers with a shoe polish tin out in the street,
My mum made tablet and toffee apples just for a treat.
Ball games, skipping ropes we were all good at that,
Singing games, chasey, we even dressed up the cat.
In a jar of water we collected rose petals off the ground,
The perfume and the colours we watched them go round and round.
Sugar-olly water is something else we made,
Liquorice pieces put in an empty lemonade bottle,
Filled with water to the top.
We had to be careful not to spill a drop.
We left it to ferment for many weeks,
Then shared it with our pals down the street.
Today's children are not safe to go out to play,
They play in each other's homes, day after day.
Computer games, the internet is the way forward
In their educational life.
If they don't get what they want
You can cut the atmosphere with a knife.
Keeping in touch with friends and parents
Is not a problem at all.
They have their mobile phones and seem to be always on call.
The younger generation today have lost their socialising skills,
I'm glad I have my memories and retrieve them at my will.

Pat McSherry

OPENING NIGHT

We've worked so hard,
for sixteen weeks.
Four months ago, we chose
our play, a play
with murder, most foul.
We decided, with great care,
our leading man in mind.
He started with us when
just a boy, blonde, shy,
with great skills, we
welcomed him to stay.
As amateurs, we've had
our ups and downs, tell me
an amateur company that doesn't.
So, in just twenty-four hours,
our curtain goes up,
the scene is Christmas Eve.
Our back stage boys, have
given us a treat, a room
with a tree and a fairy doll,
will make our patrons weep.
For the children gathered round
the tree, cannot believe
their parents, died tonight,
out on the street, by
a madman waving a gun,
fired fatal shots at them.
So now our play has begun,
Detective Page, our leading man
will see that justice is done.

Audrey Allen

FATHER

He was a good man
Taller than I am,
A lover of animals and all things kind.
When things went wrong he would just say, 'Never mind.'

He liked a drink
A pint of bitter I think.
You know he would like a smoke
Which made him a relaxed and a pleasant bloke.

Just when you thought you had an impossible problem
He would solve it by using common sense.
Gambling! Huh - he was hooked
And called all bookies crooks.

He regarded reggae music with homage
He told me many musician stories.
He could cook curried egg and rice no worries
But to taste his bacon you had to have courage.

He was seventy-four when the doctor said he'd be no more
For his type of cancer, there was no cure.
So the Angel of Death came knocking at our door
After all this is life's law.

We had the funeral three weeks ago
Everyone was at an all time low.
But we have memories and pictures to show
So we will always remember him with a warm glow.

Ali Sebastian

THE HERMIT

What happened to you hermit man
What happened in the sun
No trace of life within your shack
It seems your days are done

A boulder here, an old tin can,
The roof has even gone
A sad and lonely battered hat
Gives thought to dream upon

Was there a love within your life
Why sought you refuge here
To sit upon your lonely step
Perhaps your thoughts to clear

Although you weren't aware of it
By chance you were my friend
And gave me joy within my heart
Until the very end

I wish you well where e're you are
Please think about me too
You looked my way and smiled at me
With twinkling eyes of blue

Though evidence has gone with time
I feel your presence still
And you'll remain for ever more
My hermit on the hill

Phillippa Benson

BORN TO BE FREE

With the grass ladened
From the early morning dew.
Climb hills and vales,
Mind absorbed with the view!
For I was born to be free,
Just to wonder this land.
Some happy to be trapped,
Why they'll never understand!

Just listening to the birds,
With their early morning call.
And breathing the fresh air,
Afraid which man doth spoil!
With the sun streaming through,
Storm clouds that threat.
Sheep grazing in a field,
Not free, nor a wanted pet!

Streams trickles over rocks,
And sneaks through the undergrowth.
Deer prancing over bushes,
Enjoying freedom at its most!
Rabbits play and munch grass,
But keep a watchful eye.
Wonder back to life's demands,
Lost my freedom why I cry!

Ann Beard

GLENDALOUGH

It was summer wonders at the dawn at time
That saints, scholars, monasteries took home at Glendalough.
Between two singing lakes and wooded glen so long.

Spirits nestle in the mysterious haven
Near this sacred soil, love and labour did
Visit in one golden purpose
To serve but the holiest of holy.

Yes at Glendalough saints, scholars and chieftains
Learned the golden rule.
Oh that patience just like the trees, stones and monasteries
Is the real beauty.

Church streaming flowers of joy in a boggy glen
Light by seven angels announcing glee.
The Lamb throne upon throne
Pasture dance to the cry of a blackbird.

Tower of silver await to a Celtic dragon
Serpents, preying bats keep watch at night
Black magic, black mantras doom in this glen
Bed of angels singing alleluia to crown of ivory

The stinging evil tongues have not tasted
Or bathed in the loch Kevin's salmon flies
Reaching to a branch seven monks hymn
For the morning has broken in Glendalough.

Brian Wolohan

THE DAY WE WENT TO THE SEA

The day we went to the sea,
The gulls were wheeling and screaming above the shore,
And the sun was the hottest, they said,
For a hundred years.
And the waves came crashing down on the endless sands,
Where the children tumbled and splashed
In the rainbow spray.

Jack had been looking forward to this for weeks
He'd brought his bucket and spade,
And a floppy hat,
And a red beach ball that our gran had bought as a treat,
And he looked so fine in his stripey shirt and his shorts,
With his great big smile.

So they all ran over the sands in the blazing sun,
Laughing and teasing - young Molly,
And Ben and Jo.
And Jack's eyes were shining and he was a picture of joy,
As I wheeled him down and then carried him over the beach
To our picnic spot.

I shall never forget how he said at the end of the day,
'It's the best day I've ever had!'
And he meant it too.
Yes, the air and the sun and the laughter - they all did him good.
It's the way I remember him best, for he looked so well,
The day we went to the sea.

Jackie Lapidge

STORY OF MY LIFE

When I was child
life was so much fun.
I'd play in the garden
out in the sun.

Having a carefree life
with no worries or fears.
What more can I say
of my childhood years?

As I became a teenager,
I was in my puberty,
worried about my appearance
and how others perceived me.

I succeeded in my exams
when I was in school,
made all important decisions
without breaking too many rules.

I studied at university
far away from home,
becoming so independent
doing everything on my own.

When I graduated,
sadly, my uni years came to an end,
but, at least my useful degree
gave me a job that paid well.

Shabnam Yasmin Baz

A BLACKBIRD SITS FORLORN

A cock blackbird sits forlorn -
In that de-berried Catoniaster,
A food source must be found,
Or it's disaster.

A tractor and its entouragé
Batters past, and the underworld
Flee in abject terror.
Along the hedge-line there are spaces
Proving the farmers judgement
Sometimes is in error.

The herd of milk cows on the upper field
Graze on that November grass.
Alas it will be spring before their milk
Will have that silk - that Vanden Plas.

The beef cattle in the lower reaches
Graze the fields expanse -
And scour for roughage beneath
The river-bank beeches.

I suppose, it's with regret -
They'll not have their desired
Continental break just yet.

Alex Laird

LASTING MEMORIES

Something in the way you looked
was brought to my attention,
day after day I'd see you there
but never thought of intervention,
and then one day to my surprise
you turned and smiled my way,
suddenly the sky was blue,
oh what a lovely day.
The days went by, I'd see you there
we smiled and exchanged glances,
no words were spoken either way
each one afraid of taking chances.
The big day came, you said hello,
all I could do was stutter,
how could you know just how I felt
my heart was all a flutter.
That was many years ago
at the bus stop all in line,
who would have thought in months to come
I got my wish and made you mine.
We've walked life's path as couples do
we're stronger now than ever,
the bus stop's gone, removed from time
but we're still here together.

K Morris

OVERLAND

Overland
The carriage hurls, darkened shadows pulling reign.
Sinewed horses, steaming sweat.
Distant schedules always met. Watch it go, this hurtling train.
Overland
The carriage breaks rules of comfort, path and plan.
Painful worlds pressed with vigour,
Different dawns feel different rigour. How the pace recedes the span.
Overland
The carriage melts icy roads and frosted fields.
Galloping ground; churning round,
Bellowing found this snorting sound. Flaming hoof, no Winter yield,
Overland
The carriage slows only when the leader feeds.
Takes some quenching, purpose full.
Raise the tension, stir the lull. Steady aboard, the passenger needs.
Overland
The carriage builds strength and rapture in this wind.
Boxes weight, lifers' scope,
Knocking shoulders, bruising hope. Banking fortune's lesser sin.
Overland
The carriage stops. All the mail is read and spent.
Has the ticket claimed its fare?
Through the window space to spare. Carriage rules: *pay the rent!*

S Pete Robson

A SECRET HIDING PLACE

An elderly lady I may be
But one thing sticks in my memory:
Of many years ago
When my first beau
A gift to me he gave
And this I was to save.

I searched for a place
And found a cache
Wherein to hide my 'prize'
Away from prying eyes.

In the garden a wall of brick.
And one was loose - just the trick!
No one surely would find it there
Tucked into a space with utmost care.
I went there nearly every day
To think and while my time away.
There view my treasure - ah! So sweet
Which caused my heart to rapid beat.

My first and only 'beau' - he was ten. I was nine.
We are still together come rain or shine.
The treasured gift? I have it still - a lovely thing
In tissue paper - a curtain ring!

Patricia M Kennett

You Know You Are Alive

Sixty is no big deal
The lines on your face
Don't change.
You can do it all
Exactly as you feel
After all most of your friends
Are by now a little senile too!
They probably cannot hear, see or
Understand
So no one will notice at all.
Your bones feel no better or worse
When you wake in the morning
You know you are alive, but,
It might take gallons of tea,
To revive!
You remember the good times
And absolutely forget all the bad.
Even can exaggerate or imagine memories
That you never ever had.
But then why not indeed
Are we not a wonderful, elite
Ever increasing breed?

Vivienne Doncaster

TAN-Y-PISTYLL

Fine, silver thread among the trees,
A distant gleam midst mountains tall;
The traveller hurries on to find
A thunderous, mighty waterfall:

Tan-Y-Pistyll! Nature's might!
Sparkling spray from hilltops pour;
Over all, a rainbow's arc
Displaying work from heaven's store.

We climb around the tumbled rocks
And sense a flash of gold and blue;
Kingfisher's beauty rarely seen -
Too late - the bird is lost to view!

A deep, dark pool below the fall,
A place where brown trout love to leap.
The sunlit hillsides clothed in fern,
Each pathway made by grazing sheep.

Long years have passed since first we saw
Cambrian Mountains' treasure trove.
We love it still - and long to be
Where eagles fly and shepherds rove.

Maggie Smith

TED'S BIRTHDAY
(In The Isle Of Man)

An August day wrapped in summer blue
And just a soft, white cloud or two

A path to cycle at our ease
In company with flowers, butterflies and bees

We see Peel Hill, Corrin's Tower
Lush green fields and leafy bower

Sun sequinned water of the River Neb
The fragile beauty of a spider's web

Time to recharge the inner being
Appreciate sounds and the gift of seeing

On to St John's, Tynwald's Seat
Then the Farmer's Arms to drink and eat

Back to Peel and our harbour walk
Friends to meet and a chance to talk

A lovely sunset ends a perfect day
I'm glad we chose to spend it your way
An evening drink in the Marine - and so to bed
Many happy returns of the day dear Ted.

Joan Callister

THE SACRED PLACE

The August sun,
Beat relentlessly down,
The pair tramped on,
She, wearing a frown.

'Can't we stop here?'
Came her repeated plea,
'It's fine for a picnic
And sheltered from the sea.'

'Not much further,'
He answered with a smile,
'The place I have in mind,
Is only one more mile.'

Her heart sank deeper,
As they approached the spot,
'You'll love it here' he said,
'A place that time forgot.'

(A little later)

'Someone else has lain here,'
He uttered a plaintive cry,
'My sacred place has been defiled'
Back turned, she stifled a sigh.

Devina Symes

A SCOTS MILLENNIUM

A mist rolled in on Torridon's shore,
A lonely gull patrolled the strand
A thousand thousand years before
The Scots bestrode this ancient land.

Each clan destroyed, each weeping glen,
Each battle lost, election won.
The sum of words and deeds by Men
Can't fill the sea or dim the sun.

Take note, commemorate this Age,
But look beyond the New Year's Day.
A thousand years are but a page
Extracted from a Scottish play.

The mist will glide o'er Torridon's shore
A thousand thousand years from now
No gull will cry, the pipes no more
Will sing of battle or of plough.

A jewel-encrusted Celtic crown,
A fossil bone, a baked bean can,
A swirl of dust, like thistledown
Will mark the fleeting time of Man.

David E W Walker

BELLS OF LIFE

The smoking heap of burning stock
　of infected slaughtered cattle,
all killed because of foot and mouth
　and political tit and prattle.

The empty lane, the silent sheds,
　all devoid of moving people,
the only noise around the farm
　is from the old church steeple.

This clanging agent spreading news
　that people are around,
will give support to those in need
　from such a simple sound.

That homely, banging, ringing noise
　spreading news across the land,
that there is life outside the farm,
　a sort of helping hand.

The fields where yesterday
　the skipping woollies reign,
now are empty silent meadows,
　the flocks have all been slain.

Leslie Holgate

THE BALLAD OF RYE

I'll tell you a story,
about a man named Rye.
A thief and a highwayman,
destined to hang high.
The gallows were waiting,
should Rye ever be caught.
With a noose round his neck,
a lesson the scoundrel would be taught.
He robbed from the rich,
a pistol in his hand.
A poor boy from London,
the law could never understand.
Growing up on the streets,
orphaned at an early age.
Starvation and poverty,
filled his heart with rage.
Determined to survive,
he learned how to steal.
At the age of fourteen,
his first man he did kill.
Rye always knew in his mind one day he would die,
by the dark of night, on a lonely road.
Both pistols empty in his hands,
and no time to re-load.
When the day finally came,
Rye died fighting like a man.
Taking several troopers with him,
he fulfilled his final plan.

M A Challis

TOOTH AND PAW

I was sitting in my car having lunch one day
When I could not believe what I was seeing from afar
A weasel appeared or was it a stoat?
Dragging a tiny bunny by the throat
The only comparison I could make that day
Was of a leopard with its prey
I was too far away to interfere
Which with nature is never a good idea
How I wished for a camera to record this saga
Which was only beginning as events proved further
This was happening in the middle of the road
When suddenly the rabbit doe appeared
She took in the situation at a glance
Then she started a crazy dance
She sat up on her hind legs and started to flail
That startled killer from nose to tail
Like a boxer going for a win
What a performance she gave
As mother love and instinct took over
But alas it was all to no avail
The killer held on like grim death
All her efforts were in vain
She was forced to give up
Her struggle with nature
Now I look at rabbits with new respect
When I think of the bravery
Of that tragic Mum with the heart of a lion
Only instead of claw she only had a paw.

James Rodger

MRS DENT'S ESCAPADE

Old Mrs Dent weighed twenty-two stone
but her husband was built like a stick.
Happily she would eat all day
leaving him nothing to pick.
One day she got stuck in the bath
and all he could do was laugh,
they bought in a crane
but all was in vain
it was hopeless she just wouldn't budge.
She had to remove the bath plug
as the water soon went cold,
the poor soul shook and shivered so much
that her flab crumpled up into folds.
'Please someone help me' she yelled 'I want to get out,
I know it's my own fault for being so stout.'
Bentley the plumber came and took stock of things
'I see Mrs Dent that you've been on the binge,'
he said 'you know that you really should diet,'
Mrs Dent went very quiet,
she felt so embarrassed and very harassed,
then all of a sudden the bath was smashed,
the mess it made was terrific,
Mrs Dent looked most horrific,
to pull her up it took two hefty blokes
then as she took a step sideways she slipped on the soap
and fell down with an almighty crash,
and winded she turned rather pale
and there she lay on the lino
spread out like a gigantic whale.

Linda Beavis

BORROWDALE EXPEDITION

We came one March to Borrowdale
And it began to snow:
The morning dawned to Arctic scene
On fell, and all below!
With boots, gaiters and waterproofs,
Intrepid, and broad smile,
Through drifts up to our knees we trod
Fearless, o'er many a mile . . .
'Cross river flowing deep in spate,
Steep fell - pause for some tea -
A blizzard howled as we did wait
Chatting nonchalantly . . .
Like Yetis, on and upward strove
To reach high summit fell;
Lunch in a hollow we had dug
Inside snowdrifts, as well!
Above thick clouds in sun we bathed,
Glimpsed valley far below,
Towards stark Lakeland peaks we waved,
Soul-stirring in gleaming snow:
Like Himalayan team enthralled
By beauteous scene struck dumb,
Snowfields on hands and knees we crawled
And rubbed our fingers numb!
Gasping, we leaned on summit cairn
Jubilant, laughed out loud
As Mountain Rescue Squad waved by
And disappeared in cloud!
Two mountaineers gazed from that peak
With pride, transfixed, could hardly speak . . .

Carolyn Smith

THE BLUE ROOM

England's red rose bruised and torn,
Royalist and Cromwellian born.
A room within Cwyn Manor know,
the curse of centuries ago.
The tragedy of a fair maid, her heart
to Cavalier she gave
Bearded, handsome, laced and plumed,
rode prancing grey superbly groomed.
Slew by the sword, her lover dear,
murdered within sight of her.
Blue bedroom riven with her grief,
never a person will find sleep.
Today display Cromwellian room,
The General slept here, brought platoon.
His troops, the maiden's father led,
her brother stabbed her lover dead.
Pitiful her phantom stand, mother-to-be
no wedding band.
Repeat the horror of the maid,
all occupants become afraid.
Forever waiting, watching, seek,
her spirit by the window bleak.
Compelled the courtyard there to view,
where once her luckless lover slew.
Steep stone-topped walls, trace iron gate
the moonlight silver old Welsh slate.
Shatter the stillness, hounds find tongue,
recall the night foul deed was done.

A E Doney

Once Upon A Time

Once upon a time there was a girl of nearly forty,
She isn't really bad, just sometimes a little naughty.
She's got all these weird piercing's and a tattoo of a cute cartoon pig,
And just like her own outer shape, it's cute and very big.
This lady likes to be different, or so it would appear,
There's no need to be frightened, for she really holds no fear.
Her mum she says they're common, and her husband's not too keen,
But her children think she's funky and to them she is their queen.
It's only recently she's gone mad and has gone through pain of late,
To make herself stand out, it must be worth the wait.
The final hole's gone in now, and it's just above the lip,
It's actually called a Marilyn, and God it caused some gyp.
Her mouth swelled up and blood poured out, as the needle was
pushed in,
No pain, no gain, the piercer said, as he gave her a smirky grin.
Her hair is also metal, full of beads, an afro style,
One day she'll surely grow up, but not just for a while.
Do not judge a book by it's cover, look within to what's hidden inside,
For behind closed doors this young lady, has a job paid hourly
with pride.
Her mum is also ill now,. so she resides in the family home,
And with six children it's quite hard to find five minutes alone.
Life is very busy, being wife, carer and mum as well,
But one thing that you can positively say, she's an individual,
can't you tell?
So let's get down to the facts now, as mid-life crisis is definitely in,
It must be better than having an affair, that would be a cardinal sin.
So now my friends have you guessed yet, that this lady I mention is me,
So please accept me for what I am, and not just what you can see.

Jennifer Gleave

A SIGN OF LOVE

Christmas wasn't a time of joy
All because of a baby boy
The snow was falling pretty fast
Don't think the boy will even last

'Sir, a penny, I'll starve, I'll die
Please just one penny, for I tell you no lie'
he threw him a penny
'Now be off with your boy'

Now whilst the boy lay tired
He looked up and admired
The stars that travelled the sky
He wondered why, then started to cry

'Why do you cry?'
Asked a woman who came by
'I'm cold and all alone'
'And the pavements aren't much of a home'

Well he had a Christmas after all
And he even saw Santa Claus
That night the boy lay fast asleep
Next morning they heard not a peep

For it was time to go
And so it was told
That the young and the old
Should always behold

For this was a sign of love for a baby boy

Elias Allen

NEW BABY

When I see your tiny head, arms and legs and baby face.
It was all warm, the blood, toil and torture I faced.
I cradled you in my arms, your father in his green gown.
All the crying and temper races there
As I try not to throw my hands in the air
Rattle and dummies, bottles and bibs
Slippers and groaning, crying kid.
We celebrated your birth in full glory
All those cards mark your birth
Candles and presents and feeling unwell
Your first tooth, your first word
Throwing up all over Nanny
As poor Mum sleeps well once more
As she quietly closes the door
We love you, pet, without a doubt
So stop screaming, what's it all about?
Caring for you, loving you too
Jumping up, giving a shout
Knowing you know I'm here,
And want to mess about I fear.
Sleep tight in your bed
Think of Noddy and sleepy Ted
You know Nanny won't leave you.
Patting your face and uncreasing your gown
Now you are alone and sleeping
Once more, peace and quiet.
Isn't it swell?

A J Renyard

A MAN CALLED CODY

At dawn, Cody saddled up
Picking up his main feature,
His well-oiled rifle,
Named after the Borgia's Lucretia,
He had his rifle, close at hand
Slung across the saddle, low,
Then set out, on the railroad's behalf,
To kill the shaggy-coated buffalo,
He heard their thousand pounding hooves,
Long before he saw their rising dust,
His killing score set in his mind,
His eyes red with the murderous lust,
Cody sat calmly upon his mount,
As the herd thundered on by,
Coloured by the desert sand,
Under a white, cloudy sky,
Carefully, he took deliberate aim,
And made each shot tell,
Until he reached his highest score,
And a hundred and fifty buffalo fell,
He was an expert at the killing game,
Keeping the Chinese railroad crew fed,
That Cody soon became the top gun,
They all listened to what he said,
He ordered the skinners to skin the beasts,
Every one had been the perfect kill,
And all the world now knew this man,
By the name of 'Buffalo' Bill . . .

Gordon Bannister

A SPECIAL HOLIDAY

Five weeks in Ethiopia spent with my son
Proved to be a memorable and exciting one,
Visiting my son's fields of tèf, the national grain,
Which he was improving to prevent future starvation again.
Staying 8,000ft up in beautiful terrain,
Long hours of sunshine, and never any rain.
I had no language problem, as it is the rule,
For English to be taught to children in school.
Addis Ababa, a city contrasting old and new,
Tall modern buildings, alongside mud huts, to name but two.
Haile Selassie's Parliament, glass panels portraying life,
In Africa, before communist onslaught and strife.
Emperor Menelik's abode, his regalia on display,
Jewelled robes, and three-tiered crown, in splendid array.
Staying overnight at Rift Valley Game Park where I saw,
Many rare animals, baboons and exotic birds galore.
At British Embassy, private apartments I viewed,
Served with afternoon tea, my spirits renewed.
Attending their garden party celebrating Armistice Day,
In a wonderful garden bright with floral display.
Visiting a famous leprosy hospital where patients learn
To spin, weave and embroider, their living to earn.
Seeing roadside tents which remain for a week,
For relatives and mourners, as solace they seek.
I learned that the coffee bean we take for granted,
Originated in Ethiopia, before being overseas planted.
Old churches with painted murals, distinctive and rare,
Depicting biblical scenes and guarded with fanatical care.
Seeing the statue of St George on main thoroughfare.
Strange to think that Ethiopia, our patron saint we share.

E Kathleen Jones

THE BURNING BUSH

One day as I kept
My father-in-law's flock
I led the flock to
The back of the desert;
I passed by the mountain of God
Even to Horeb
I dreaded and stood in awe
This is one of the many days
Day by day I trod this path
But that day, the angel of the Lord
Appeared to me in a flame of fire
Out of the midst of a bush
And I looked and
Behold the bush burned
With fire and the bush
Was not consumed
Then I said, I will now turn aside
And see this great sight
Why the bush is not burned
Then I heard a voice
Calling unto me out of
The midst of the bush and said
Here am I
He began to talk with me saying
Draw not nigh hither;
Put off your shoes from off your foot
For the place whereon you stand
Is a holy ground
I hid my face for I was afraid
To look upon Him.

Ebenezer Essuman

MY DAY

The tide was coming in the bay,
And the path before me lay.
As I set off, over stile and hill,
New pastures to roam, what a thrill.
Sky of blue, gentle breeze,
Whole day to do as I please.
Not a care or worry here,
No work or chores today my dear.
Elevenses! Time to sit and eat,
Even found myself a seat.
Flask of coffee, choc biscuit too,
While sat gazing at the view.
Time to press on over stile again,
Giving entry to a lane.
This leads me down to beck and mill,
Now disused and long since still.
Village green with pub calls me,
With ploughman's lunch under chestnut tree.
Twelve pm, half the day gone,
Think I will stop here till it's one.
Had a little doze here too,
Now I've woke it's nearly two.
So better get upon my way,
Few more miles to do today.
Through the meadow, by lambs and sheep,
Who stare, then run and jump and leap.
Now my route is very plain,
Over the hill, and down again.
Back to shore I roam,
And the path along the beach to home.

G W Bailey

ROBERT

Dark hills silhouetted against the sky,
The wind whistles in the trees,
I hear the whinny of the horse
Then its hooves, as horse and rider go by.

They flew like the wind,
The horse and the child,
Moving as one
Both hearts on fire.

The child rode bareback
No saddle or reins,
Or shoes on his feet,
Both heels tucked in to share the heat.

A thing of beauty
They were as they came,
The boy's head right down
As he clung to its mane.

His eyes were alight
With the thrill of the race,
And my heart filled with pride
When I gazed on his face.

A free spirit he was
Who didn't know fear,
As he rode with the horse
With no fancy gear.

I will always remember
The horse and the child,
And the love that they shared
Out there in the wild.

Joan May Wills

I'LL TELL YOU A TALE

You ask me what I used to be
Sit here lad, and I'll tell you a tale
Of the time I sailed the stormy sea
To fight against a roaring gale.

We left the bay, on the morning tide
The breeze was fresh, the sea was calm
Before us stretched the ocean wide
With the sky so blue, the sun so warm

For days we sailed with nothing in view
Then the rain came down, the wind grew strong
You could tell by the look on the faces of the crew
They sensed there was something wrong

Eight bells and all is well
Then suddenly we heard a roar
The waves began to rise and swell
Over the ship they started to soar

Men were swept along at will
The sound of thunder filled the sky
Lightning flashed, with a strength to kill
Some of my mates, too young to die

I prayed to God to spare my life
Please let this storm soon pass
I think about my lonely wife
As I kiss the picture of my lass

Well, here I am to tell the tale
So, I'll tell you what I used to be
Because those seas, no more I'll sail
A swarthy pirate, that was me.

Grace Wallace

WITH THE TOSS OF DAWN

Steeple clocks strike the hour of waking time:
The city hubbub blinks a new but sleepy eye.
With the toss of dawn comes the chatter of birds -
a prelude to the rising sounds of the commerce city.
(Docklands - where tall cranes to the clouds hide -
constantly squeal with the harshness of the stevedore's craft:
Plimsoll lines bob in the murkiness of the oily water-basin.)

Urban suburbs disturb the sleeping dust of night, when,
at fitful rest, love and dreams toyed fancifully
and pillows absorbed the sobs of those with sorrow, with contrition . . .

Ambitious industry withdraws the bolts of its doors
as workers phlegmatically leave for the day's toil
to earn the means to exist and for hopeful fulfilment.

The quiescence of the night soon loses its fresh rejuvenation,
when workers and machines commence slavishly, regardlessly,
                                        unknowingly
polluting the air with cacophony and that malady called - asthma.

But, somewhere there are havens - always a haven:
amongst those remaining remnants of the natural world:
a wild woodland? - untouched, as yet, by the spread of Man
(or there is little point in presence just for toil).

Timepieces tediously bore away day's awoken time,
unaware of what time is and -
unconcerned for man's often droll and humdrum pursuits.

Seconds make minutes - minutes build hours that tumble unopposed,
                                        unchallenged
until the dust of night returns to fall, settle,
and make playful dreams and damp pillows,
until, yet again, with the toss of dawn,
steeple clocks strike the hour of waking time.

William G Thomas

ARE YOU MY DADDY?

As I strolled along a country lane
On a bright midsummer's day
I paused at the gate of a mansion house
To watch small children at their play

The sign on the gate said 'Children's Home'
And as I wondered how could this be
I became aware of two big brown eyes
Staring through that gate at me

The face of a little angel
With her cheeks all wet with tears
Cried 'Please tell me you're my daddy
And you've come to take me home from here.'

I knelt down and held that little hand
That she stretched out to me
And like her my face was wet with tears
As I sought the way to let her see

That I am just a travelling man
And like her, no family of my own
But although I was not her daddy
Didn't mean she was alone.

For everywhere that I will travel
And through my grief how dark the night
I'd think of her in all her innocence
And her little face would be the light

I pray that someone takes the little girl
And makes for her a home
And that a mummy and a daddy
Will give her the love she'd never known.

Don Woods

STOWAWAY

A ship she stands bound for Amerikey,
To the land of cotton, land of the free,
Sailing with her cargo,
That's meant for Wells and Fargo,
While deep inside the hull,
I spy a close-cropped skull,
It is of a petite gamin,
Escaping from Ireland's potato famine,
And from poverty, away from Mammon
He gave the guards on quay the slip,
So as he could stow away aboard ship,
No need to explain,
Until they reach the port of Maine,
Hopes high, not in vain
With good fortune embedded in his brain,
To the wheelhouse he'll steal,
And try to poach an honest meal,
So on the deck he lingered,
Pickpocket, able-fingered,
This half-starved waif, as light as a cork,
Hoping to make his fortune in New York,
Work hard - make billions,
Maybe even millions,
Come back and buy up Ireland,
And call it my land
Then well fed and secure,
Blow a raspberry on being poor,
So Stowaway
Hide from light of day
Till you reach Amerikey,
Where a new life begins for me.

Alan Pow

IN BRAYDON WOOD

Something was up
in Braydon Wood.

Trees winter-brooded
in silence,
a spotted woodpecker
looped from
branch to branch;
hares made for
the open field
and a deer crashed
through the
undergrowth,
white bob-tail
flashing.

By thick trunk
of Wellingtonia,
the hunt was gathered,
cars glittering
like sabres
on the grass.

Tap, tap . . . went hazel
stick against green boot,
whilst a line of menace
beat the undergrowth . . .

Tip-toe, tip-toe,
the pheasants passed
behind their ranks.

On Braydon pond,
a duck laughed.

Sue Chadd

THE FRAUDSTER

Our colleague, object of pity,
Eyesight rapidly failing,
Groping short-sightedly around the school,
Living with slatternly wife and brood in rundown cottage.
Even our charges felt sorry for him.

Six months on, complaints from retailers,
Bills unpaid for furniture and bedding.
A furious headmaster, fearful for the institution's reputation,
Retained part of his salary, clearing what debts he could.

He departed with a flurry of bouncing cheques,
To milkman, village pub, coal merchant, newsagents,
'What gall,' the latter said. 'The bank was closed.
I took his cheque to pay my bill and give him extra cash.
Just worthless paper.'

He fled to another village.
Warnings sped to traders there.
Too late, he'd struck with lightning speed,
Enmeshing them in his uncreditworthy web.

News came that in his previous post,
He'd been the guardian of the pupils' spending money.
Inspired appointment!
He used the funds for wagers,
Till horses lost their form and boys their tuck.

Two large, tight suited gentlemen enquired his whereabouts.
'He hasn't paid his bookie - bad mistake,' an Irish master said,
One of the betting crowd.

Our thick lensed fraudster disappeared,
Such people do.
No doubt he leeched more innocent communities.

Peter Hicks

DANCING WITH FATHER NEPTUNE

I know not when I was born but it was in the dawning of time,
my place of birth buried deep within the myths of Cornish lore,
but I emerged in a gentle bubbling stream, rising from the depths
where the womb of Mother Earth lay well hidden from prying eyes.
Trembling and eager to explore I began my journey into the unknown,
wary of what I would find on my endless quest to see my journey's end.
As I slid within the twists and turns of my long, snaking river
I grew heady and unheeding of any danger that might wait ahead,
flowing faster and faster in exultant anticipation,
impatient to unravel the awe-inspiring mysteries that seemed to beckon.
I roughly probed the dark and hidden crevices, eerie and chilling,
some frozen in the cruel and icy grip of harsh winter,
then rose on the swell of the tide to greet the summer sun
sparkling and shimmering like golden gauze on my laughing wavelets.
As I grew stronger and bolder I sprinted in leaps and bounds,
skipping the stones and jumping the rocks as high as I could,
then tumbling and weaving crazy patterns in my excitement,
wanting to reach each curling twist and bend to find I knew not what,
but something drew me ever onward as though on a silver string
seeming to rise and fall to the rhythm of fluting notes in the crystal air.
Then the soaring melody grew wilder and wilder and I was in a frenzy,
desperate to find whatever was calling to me from the mists
                                                    of the future.
Becoming more exhausted until I could bear the wait no more
I burst forth upon the endless seas in a huge explosion of exaltation
and knew that at last I had reached my final destination.
In a paroxysm of ecstasy I joined the everlasting oceans,
embracing and enfolding them within my flailing, seething arms,
my destiny to forever glide the endless swell beneath infinite skies,
never to return to flow between the hills and valleys
                                                    from whence I sprung.
As I circled the earth in my continuous dance with Father Neptune
I pined for Cornwall, the beautiful and mysterious land of my birth,
forever lost to me as I ebbed and flowed till the end of time.

Paddy Jupp

VENUS TO VEGAS

Zeemo came from Venus
In a brand-new rocketship,
He fancied a vacation -
A little cosmic trip.

He landed north of Moscow
This was not quite his plan,
The cold near froze his clonkies
And no chance of a tan!

He took off for the Congo
It must be hotter there,
But came down in the heart of Rome -
Right in St Peter's Square.

The Pope rushed out to greet him
The people knelt to pray,
Then Zeemo got emotional
And asked if he could stay.

After a week of resting
He waved goodbye to Rome
And planned to visit Washington
Before returning home.

He stopped off in old England
But didn't like the rain,
So he loaded up with tea and cakes
And then took off again.

A storm blew up from nowhere
Then everything went black,
He crashed just outside Roswell
And never made it back . . .

. . . Zeemo now lives happily in Las Vegas
And is a big fan of Frankie Avalon!

Cavan Magner

THE DRIVING SAGA

Driving experience came in a rush,
devoid of knowledge of gears and clutch.
First gear selected, I jerked down the road, tiger in tank.
Did I say 'Tiger?' It was a large kangaroo,
with my husband shouting 'Silly old moo.'
Stop at 'major road ahead', other wise we both are dead.
An unwary cyclist in flowing cape,
visibly paled and started to gape.
He pushed on his pedals, a foot from my bonnet
I jammed on the brake and luckily made it!
As I entered the road with a kangaroo jump,
the cyclist dismounted with a heavy thump.
I thought myself to be in clover,
when a driving instructor took me over.
'It's really easy, child's play' he said as
conflicting thoughts entered my head.
I turned the car round, still in one piece,
to the instructor a happy release.
'Now I think we will try some reversing,
I will get out and do the observing.
In my manic frame of mind, I noticed he kept behind
I mounted the pavement and ran over his toes
He tottered back in and my nerves just froze.
The manoeuvre to master, I had to relent,
Then one day we made another attempt
'Perhaps you're not ready,' he wisely observed,
his patience already held in reserve.
I feel further practice is now required,
this is exactly what I feared
The months passed by, I was entered for test
instructor's opinion, 'Dodgy at best'.
By a miracle I managed to pass,
as my friends said in unison, 'Really, at last!'

Cynthia Briggs

My Story

That young woman in the cage
She couldn't remember her name or age
Locked away for three weeks long
Nobody knew just what went wrong.

No desire for food, she was forcefully fed
Held down by others surrounding her bed
Brought back to reality by the shock of it all
'I'll eat, I'll eat' was her pitiful call.

She had searched for something she couldn't find
Man-made doctrine brought no peace of mind
She believed what was said by those nice young men
Never once did she see the lion's den.

Wanting nothing to do with 'religion' any more
Determinedly she locked that door
Months passed and the clock was ticking away
Yet Jesus still watched her every day.

One night in a dream she travelled to a place
Jesus was there, and she saw His face
Shocked by the love and compassion she saw
With a loud cry she fell to the floor.

Many years were to pass before the Lord called her name
Then tenderly He touched her soul once again
Suddenly one day she knew for sure
She was unsaved and so spiritually poor.

Today I thank Jesus for what He has done
I worship the Father, the Spirit, the Son
I don't understand why They bothered with me
Yet here I am, unchained and set free
Living proof that Jesus is faithful and true
Yes, He died on that cross for me and for you.

Desiree Knoesen

A LITTLE OF WHAT YOU FANCY

There are times when things turn out
In such a way that leaves no doubt
That it's impossible to know
When good deeds can rebound, and so
Is the tale that I now tell,
When, instead of staying at an hotel,
We spent our holiday abroad
With German friends. We had free board
So we took gifts for them instead:
Some porcelain and Scottish shortbread,
Together with a box of sweets -
And in addition to these treats,
Some dog-chocs for the family pet,
Which, later on, we would regret.
One day, when we returned to base,
Of dog-chocs there was no trace.
When we opened the tin, we found
Nothing left. We looked around
Yet the tin, with lid intact,
Was on the table. No dog could extract
A choc and then replace the lid -
Oh, no, we were not so stupid!
Our friend's wife came in from the kitchen,
Having stayed behind to cook a chicken
For our evening meal. She was shamefaced.
When told what she had eaten, braced
Herself for upset stomach, but all
That happened was her husband, Karl,
With misguided sense of humour,
Barked at her - what a bloomer!

B Gordon

SCOTLAND'S LIVING HISTORY

Forget history books, so dull and so cold,
Just sit back and listen as tales I unfold.
Such colourful characters take centre stage,
From short times of peace, to when battles rage.
There's Macbeth, and warriors, like Wallace and Bruce,
All out to win, with no talk of a truce.
Their swords paved the way for honour and might,
Telling all Scots to stand up, and fight.
Queen Mary, caught up in life's cruel fate,
Found herself at Traitors Gate.
Revenge came, when Elizabeth, childless, died,
For then Mary's son James was not denied
His claims to the throne of England, too,
And under him harmony blossomed and grew.
Now Bonny Prince Charlie arrives on the scene -
Oh, what a fine king *he* would have been!
So gallant, so young - but 'twas not to be -
He fled to Skye, rowed over the sea.
And Flora MacDonald who helped him then
Is surely a name all Scots will ken.
There's a castle in Stirling, grandiose and old
How many tales its stones could have told!
You feel it in the atmosphere whenever you go there,
The past just seems to come alive, it's in the very air.
You scent the ghosts of Mary, James and many others, too
(was it *they* who passed you by, or just the wind that blew?)
So, visit Stirling's Old Town, and its castle on the hill,
And listen to its 'voices' that seem to echo still.
Up there is 'living' history, far better than a book,
So why not come and listen - or simply have a look?

Joyce Hockley

TREASURE BLESSED

Our Charlie is a boy of three
whose hair curls inconceivably
in spirals and cascading waves
of gold and blonde in varied shades.

His almond eyes of chestnut brown
would wipe away the deepest frown.
With chubby cheeks and nose so pert
in later years he's bound to flirt
with all the girls, who will for sure
fall all about him by the score.
Dismayed when they are told by Char,
he'd rather tinker with his car
than dance the night away with girls
in frilly frocks and strings of pearls.

But just for now he must endure
the trials of being nearly four.

Blessed with looks of a cherubim
folks will insist he's not a him.
To which he stamps his feet and shouts
'I'm not a girl' . . . then starts to pout.
It won't last long, a smile breaks through
and now he's got them smiling too.
Endearing ways, angelic face,
devilish mischief wrapped in lace . . .
sugar and spice, there is no doubt
is not what boys are all about.

Daughters . . . why with a son so cute?
(Though gender may be in dispute!)
The love that shines through eyes so bright
make him a child of pure delight.

Susan Seward

THE MARINER'S ARMS

The Mariner's Arms, A Cautionary Tale
Starting when the brewery put her up for sale.
The regulars cried as all their traditions died
When the brewery made changes to bring in new trade
Leaving so many people feeling deeply betrayed.
Out went sea-shanties and legends of mermaids.
In came a jukebox and inexperienced barmaids.
Out went the landlord, like flotsam and jetsam.
In came theme nights like Country and Western.
Out went an excellent choice of real ales
In come over-priced silly names for cocktails.
The Yuppified businessmen cruelly taunted
Claim that The Mariner's Arms was haunted
By a sailor's wife who took her own life
On learning that he was lost at sea
In circumstances that history
Logs as something of a mystery.
There were protests and even a petition
But the brewers replied with only derision
Describing the changes as economic decision.
The opening night was one of celebration,
Dancing and drinking and much jubilation,
But there was a girl at the back with tears in her eyes
And not one of the rich pissheads seemed to recognise
Her strange resemblance to the lady in the portrait
Until for them, it was already far too late.
They murdered Karaoke all night long
Until the pale siren sang her sad song,
Her very own special and mournful request
Turning Mariner's Arms to Marie Celeste.

Arthur Chappell

STRAND OF EVIDENCE

One hazy dawn I strolled along
a shallow beach. The tide had gone
and left an unmarked plain it seemed
that no one else had trodden on.

Then at the ripples' edge I saw
the tracks of two who'd gone before -
companions walking side by side,
together matching every stride;
the larger shoe with measured tread
restrained so not to get ahead.

And to their pleasant course I kept,
though never stepping where they'd stepped.
I noticed that the smaller feet
were showing an uneven beat.
Perhaps the rubbing of a shoe
had caused a limp that left this clue.

Then further on both paused to face,
and after that there was no trace
of smaller feet, but just one track
as stronger carried weaker back,
with deeper dents and staggered gait
as evidence of extra weight,
until they reached the soft, dry sand
where countless feet had trudged inland.

And there the pair were lost to me,
so I turned back towards the sea
to watch the tide creep quickly in
and clear all signs of where we'd been:
beneath the water's sparkling screen
no proof remained of what I'd seen.

Patricia Farley

RUPERT TRANSFORMED

Whimpering tiny blob of black,
Umbilical cord attached,
Poachers brought him in a sack -
Whose mother they had just despatched!

Dropper, then by bottle fed,
Crying for food day and night,
His body grew to match his head,
Peaceful when his belly's tight.

The children took the job of weaning
With fruit and mushy rice,
Mother-like his soft fur cleaning,
Played with him . . . at some price.

Outgrowing all, his fearsome claws,
Weapons to offset his breed's short sight.
A den was made for him outdoors,
But he escaped to the house at night.

At length Rupert was a full-grown bear
Ready to return to normal life -
Moved to a forest settlement, where
It was hoped he'd find himself a wife.

At first he came back for each meal,
Although enjoying jungle walking,
Rangers behind him would steal
Taking notes quietly stalking.

He found a girl, pursued with care,
He was gauche, she magnanimous,
So Rupert once a petted bear
Became 'Helarctos Malayanus'.

Di Bagshawe

THE ROMANTIC

I had this nice young boyfriend.
Thought for me there'd be no other.
But when I met his family,
I fell for his big brother.

He's not like his younger sibling.
He's more handsome and much sexier.
But he always gets his words mixed up
Because he's got dyslexia.

Another thing about him:
He's left-handed, but that's fine.
I just think it makes him special,
And I want to make him mine.

I know that he loves me as well,
Each day he sends a note.
And most times I know what he means
In spite of what he wrote.

In yesterday's love letter,
He told me he thinks I'm swet,
And wants to sski my lovely lisp
The next time we can met.

I told him we should run away
To Ireland, on the ferry.
He wrote, 'I'd rather Greetna Gren,
'It's you I went to merry!'

So, if he can read the road signs,
And we don't drive up to Loch Ness,
We've decided we'll elope
And live our lives in wadded bless!

Linda Burnel

CUBA

*(Dedico ésta poema a mis compadres
Cubanos - en particular Vladamir)*

I feel like an alien in my own town
Life here is never going to be the same
Now that I've fallen in love
With hot, dirty, crazy Havana.

The days blurred into one
The nights were endless
The laughter incessant
The bond with Havaneros unbreakable.

I loved the danger -
being stopped by police because
we hung around with Cubanos.

I loved being stuck in a Russian-style hotel
lift in Santa Maria del Mar
knowing warm turquoise waves
were waiting for me outside.

I loved eating black beans and rice
by candlelight,
watching my new friends using
cigarette lighters to see their meals,
used to regular power cuts.

I loved taking the rickety ferry boat
over the harbour of Havana
and standing by the statue of Christ,
overlooking my wonderful new home.

I dream about Cuba every night
I wish I hadn't left my heart and soul there.

Anon

SAM

I found our Sam huddled in a corner of a disused rubbish dump.
He lay there whimpering, he looked a poor pathetic lump.
I slowly went to him and said
'Come on little chap, let me take you home into the warm,
                      where you can have a little nap.'
He shyly comes to me and gives his tail a gentle wag
His eyes begin to brighten, gone is the look that was so sad
I whips my belt off from my old mac
Slips it round his neck and starts to stroke his back.
He looks up at me, pleased with the bit of affection shown
So I coax him out and along the road we head towards home
But my old lady ain't too gay
When I explain the little chap is here to stay.
She starts to moan about the puddles round the house
Then I knew, she'd have to have her grouse.
Soon that little chap is well settled in
He's full of bounce, vigour and vim
A good plain name we decide for this young man
So it has to be just 'Sam'.
I take him along to the local vet
Who gives him a jab in the back of the neck
Vet says to me 'You've got a fine young dog'
As our Sam stands there, still as a log.
Our Sam grows and starts to put on weight
You should see him eat and lick his plate
A dog disc my old lady rushes out and buys
'I don't want the law round here,' she cries.
Very soon our Sam starts to learn a thing or two
How to sit and beg and chase next door's cat on cue.
I know he's going to be the best mate I could own
And I'll make him happy
'Cos from now on, he'll never be alone.

Shirley Webster

FUN TIME

The daylight has faded and shadows now fall
And the moon creeping through sheds its light over all.
It's time, now the day's work is over and done,
To dress up and join in with the crowd having fun
And wend our way down to the bright lights in town
Where the night life awaits, and we let our hair down.

The music and discos are throbbing with sound
And so many people are milling around
Arriving in taxis and sleek polished cars
For the musicals, dance floors, night clubs, and lounge bars -
The restaurants are busy - booked tables await
The arrival of guests on their celebration dates.

There's action as well where the teenagers eat
In the coffee bar shop where they all like to meet,
Down the road take away snacks, and hot dog stall queues,
And the street corner vendor calling out 'Evening news',
Loyal film fans are streaming through cinema swing doors,
While theatre shows await curtain calls and applause.

Everyone's having fun and the atmosphere's great,
And boys and girls meet on that romantic date,
It's the time for us all to relax and enjoy
Because in our hearts, each, lurks a fun girl or boy -
But the night life, it seems, all too quickly slips by
And the bright lights give way to the star studded sky.

The last waltz is over, the shows have closed down,
The streets are deserted it's so quiet now in town
For the crowds are all wending their way home again
By taxi or coach, or fast speeding train,
And the moon, now descending bids 'Goodnight everyone',
Soon dawn will be breaking, a new day has begun.

F Evelyn D Jones

COTTAGE ON THE HILL

You once stood proud upon the hill
Rose Cottage was your name.
Though long gone I remember still,
That day the bulldozers came.

Your whitewashed walls sheltered me,
From the raging storm.
Blazing log fire welcomed me,
Kept me snug and warm.

Sparkling panes at your windows,
Gleamed with jewelled light.
Quaint shutters rattling in the breeze,
Kept out the cruellest night.

A straw thatched roof with chimney tall,
Drifting smoke I still recall.
I still smell roses round your door,
But they are gone, they are no more.

Gone for all eternity.
Machines took you away from me,
And as I sit here and wait,
All that's left is a broken gate.

No more roses round your door,
No more to tread your stone flagged floor.
No more the smell of fresh baked bread,
But you are with me, inside my head.

They took your pride, memories too,
But come what may I'll remember you.
For wherever in the world I roam,
In my heart you are still my home.

Josie Rawson

AUNT WIN (1882-1965)

They say Aunt Win had been a pretty child;
She grew into a beauty, and drove men wild.
It started when she was swept off her feet
By a handsome young man who lived in the street.
He may have been handsome, but seemed a bit dim,
So Auntie Win very quickly get tired of him.

Then she posed for an artist, in the nude;
Her family were furious, and thought it rude.
The trouble was that she could see no harm,
If gentlemen enjoyed her natural charm.
She had this string of men in her life
But, none of them ever called her wife.

Flighty Aunt Win kept changing her mind,
But didn't want her lovers to think her unkind.
This led to a situation, most confusing,
Which some tittered at, and found amusing;
For Aunt Win was in the family way
And, I can tell you, there was hell to pay.

The family said she's brought them shame,
Bearing a child that had no name.
The year was nineteen hundred and two,
And Aunt Win's choices were very few.
She went to a town where she wasn't known,
And gave birth to her daughter, all alone.

Aunt Win decided to call the baby Pearl,
And found a foster mother for her little girl.
The child was taught to call her mother, Auntie Win,
And never knew she'd been conceived in sin.
So, you see, in 1965, when Aunt Win died,
Pearl didn't know it was for her mother that she cried.

Geraldine Parr

PANDEMONIUM

Who am I?
Which image is real?
Shutters click, I pose
Responding to this deal.
They point their cameras
I put on a show,
Creating pandemonium
Every trick in the book I know.

Seeking attention
That is my lifeblood.
Wrap them around my fingers
Cos it makes me feel good.
Pouting posing
Strutting my stuff,
Dazzle like diamonds
They can't get enough.

What will happen next?
Fame will go by
So long I've had you, fame
Fame is a flame
That flickers then dies.
This fickleness of fortune
Forever reaching for the moon,
Then crashing back to Earth
Former friends giving a wide berth.

All my life I've been searching
Searching endlessly,
Searching for a missing person
That missing person is me.

Ian Barton

TIA

Your coat is as soft as the silk
That spiders have spun
And golden, my beautiful pup
As corn in the sun.

As brown as a deep mountain tarn
Are your bright, pleading eyes
So thoughtful - although what you think
I can only surmise.

It seems that you sense my return
For some minutes before
I appear, for whenever I come
You are there at the door.

And barking a welcome so warm
That I can't but be glad.
A dearer companion than you
No one ever had.

As you sport with the waves on the shore
'Neath a blue April sky
Or go bounding ahead through the woods
When the bracken is high

Or race in the Fall up the hills
That the heather makes bright
Or walk silently under the stars
On a clear, frosty night.

Or try catching the flakes as they fall
When the world's under snow -
My Tia, you give me more joy
Than you ever could know.

Emma Kay

A BLACKBIRD CALLED RYE

Up on high soars a blackbird called Rye
Keeping an eye over a town gone by
An old guy walks by with a lie
Then the blackbird called Rye breathes a sigh
Asks him why he walks with a lie
The guy looks up with a solemn reply
For tonight I fear I have to die
The blackbird called Rye asks him why
The guy tells the blackbird called Rye
And with a tear in his eye he starts to cry
But walks on with his head up high
As he leaves he straightens his tie
He wishes good evening to the blackbird called Rye
Now Rye continues with a sparkle in his eye
Over the town he continues to spy
The blackbird called Rye thinks oh my
As he looks on down over a hot pie
Now the pie is cooling thinks Rye
A missing ingredient thinks young Rye
He then sees the old guy
And not wanting to beg nor pry
Questions what's missing from this pie
As before he whispers to Rye
No matter how hard you try
You are the missing ingredient from the pie
The blackbird called Rye asks the guy
Do you speak with the truth or lie
How many ingredients go into the pie
Four and twenty replies the guy
Above his head is a knife up high
Rye does realise it's time to die
The guy releases a laugh loud and sly
And he who holds the mystery of the blackbird called Rye
Who was never seen again

Jamie Barnes

APOLLO ELEVEN

The countdown reached zero. All systems were 'Go'
As the Saturn's great engines began
And rocketed skyward a manned lunar craft.
The ultimate dream known to man.
The lift-off was perfect and carried aloft
Three privileged men of our race.
Apollo eleven then soared out of sight,
Continuing on into space.

Mike Collins, 'buzz' Aldrin and Neil Armstrong knew,
As they rode on that pillar of fire,
The perilous mission entrusted to them
And their chance to achieve man's desire.
When in lunar orbit the Eagle cast off
And both Aldrin and Armstrong were sent
On the very last stage of their fantastic flight
As the capsule began its descent.

'The Eagle has landed.' The message came through
As the vessel came safely to rest.
Then Armstrong emerged in his cumbersome suit
About to be put to the test.
As Armstrong descended, the watchers on earth
Were eagerly waiting to see
The first steps of man on an alien world
In the Sea of Tranquillity.

The tension had mounted from hour to hour,
But the whole mission climaxed as soon
As the astronaut lowered himself from LEM
And placed his left foot on the moon.
The frontier of space had been conquered at last
And man's earthbound days left behind,
As Armstrong declared 'That's one small step for man;
One giant leap for mankind!'

Dennis Turner

CHARLIE THE RABBIT

Has many a habit,
Some good
And some naughty;

Diddler the tabby puss,
Who always cries to get a fuss,
Is her friend
And they chase the other cats,
Whoever gets in their way;

She hops and skips,
But when she gets mad,
She stamps about
And may give,
Humbug a clout;

Billy's sweet rabbit mixture,
Comes up tops,
But her favourite treat,
Are lots and lots of Pips rabbit drops,
No other can beat;

She likes other things too,
Cucumber, carrots, to name a few;

Her neighbour, Maltezer,
Is a guinea pig,
A very timid one,
He likes a cuddle,
But to catch him is a struggle;

Owen the kitten,
He's a terror,
He loves to play in the cellar;

Bubbles is his mum,
She is glad she only had one.

Jane Milthorp

SEEMED TO ADDRESS

You see,
You start from innocence,
To arrive back;
In innocence.

These the words,
Of grandpa Palermo;
As he gazed,
Into the fiery horizon.

Wouldn't think,
Was initiating,
Grandchild;
Cross-legged,
On sands of time.

Seated on rock,
Proud of texture and hue;
Seemed to address,
The horizon.
The fiery, horizon.

Lord have mercy!
The gentleman,
Who, on entering a club;
Old brandy,
Straight up, Charlie!

Why not,
Orange juice, if you may;
In the private knowledge,
Mature complement, inevitable.

The sun sailing, in free expanse,
Lessoning, on economy;
Wisdoms, in restraint.

Rowland Warambwa

THE RIVER'S STORY

Close where iris skirts the water
Heron makes but one request
That within this perfect haven
She may build her cosy nest
As the breeze skims through the rushes
Tiny vole will shyly peep
Stirring not those downy bundles
Where young water-hens seek sleep
Bulrush thrives on mossy island
Where forget-me-nots are rife
Adding to the river's splendour
As she hastens on through life
Onward, onward flows her current
Granting every springtime wish
Laughing as that king of bird life
Dives on unsuspecting fish
Weeping willow trails her tresses
Where the bank is soft and low
As the swallows swoop in circles
Watching river's tireless flow
But the sights and sounds she savours
Are a source of rich delight
Wending her eventful journey
Hour by hour through day and night
See now as that swan emerges
Gliding proudly round the bend
Yes indeed the river's story
Once begun shall have no end.

Juliet C Eaton

SUBMISSIONS INVITED
SOMETHING FOR EVERYONE

POETRY NOW 2001 - Any subject,
any style, any time.

WOMENSWORDS 2001 - Strictly women,
have your say the female way!

STRONGWORDS 2001 - Warning!
Age restriction, must be between 16-24,
opinionated and have strong views.
(Not for the faint-hearted)

All poems no longer than 30 lines.
Always welcome! No fee!
Cash Prizes to be won!

Mark your envelope (eg *Poetry Now) 2001*
Send to:
Forward Press Ltd
Remus House, Coltsfoot Drive,
Peterborough, PE2 9JX

**OVER £10,000 POETRY PRIZES
TO BE WON!**

Judging will take place in October 2001